CONSIDER THE CREATOR

Seeing God in all that has happened, all that is happening, and all that will happen.

CONTENTS

Dedication

YOU. This book is dedicated to you.
God led me, someone who, by the world's standard was not equipped to write a book, to write this for YOU. I don't have a huge following on social media, I don't have hundreds of thousands of marketing dollars, I just have the ability to merge my testimony with scripture in hopes that ONE single soul would read this and it would lead them to TRULY, ONCE AND FOR ALL, surrender their life to Christ. YOU… The person who searches everywhere for peace but has been avoiding the Bible. The person who believes their life is a series of being the back seat passenger, never playing an important role in someone else's life. The person who was/is abused physically and verbally and thinks that life is about rolling with the punches because you're "weak". The person who goes through life feeling rejected by everyone and feels like they fail at everything. The person who has experienced church hurt and has blamed God for the acts of flawed humans. The person who runs from their calling because the idea they had for their life is less scary and seems more fun. The person who has called themselves Christian for years but the fruits aren't there. The person who loves unconditionally but is slowly becoming more and more discouraged because you feel like the love you give doesn't matter. The person who has been blessed enough to reach their elder years and has forgotten that we're supposed to be running the race

Until the end, I hope this book helps reignite your faith. The person who is firm in faith, but there are no others around you who truly desire to live a faithful and obedient life. The person who is a "baby christian" and has no clue what this walk is about.

This book is for you…

Introduction

I'm glad you're here. I'm glad God found it necessary for you to come to this earth and dwell amongst us at this time. Your existence matters. In fact, your existence matters tremendously. Thank you for being here with us and thank you for picking up this book that I have poured many years of experiences, hours of reflecting, months of mourning and several weeks at a time asking God "why?".

This is the first book I've written and it actually took me over three years to complete. The last two months of writing is the only period of the time where I was confident about what I was putting on these pages. I kept telling myself "you're not an author" and "you don't even know how to use punctuation properly and you jumble your words too much" but God gave me the strength, and the Holy Spirit worked through me to put all these experiences and thoughts together.

The turning point in the last two months of this writing process happened when the Lord took me back to an experience I had in seventh grade. I always had bad grades throughout the semesters, but I would find a way to convince my teachers to let me turn in late work so that my grade would at least get up to a C-. In seventh grade I had a teacher that was a force to be reckoned with, Mr. Landers. I went to him one day at the end of the semester to work my charm, but

I quickly realized I had met my match. After a few firm words and some long silences with that fatherly eye contact, he told me the only way I will be able to get my grade up is if I wrote an essay on why he should raise my grade up and what I wanted to do with my life… So, I wrote the essay. I believe it was around 5 to 6 pages long and to be completely honest with you, I don't even remember everything I wrote. A few days after I turned it in he pulled me out to the hallway. I could see a look on his face that I had never seen before. He looked me deep in my eyes and said "I got the essay you wrote. It was good. In fact, it was so good that I almost made you stand up in front of the class and read it." That meant a lot coming from a guy like him. I don't remember what happened after this and I never saw the essay ever again. I came to realize it's not the details of the essay that mattered in this moment of reflection. The Lord took me back so I could see that He actually did give me the ability to write things down, and those things have the ability to deeply move people. He led me to see that I've had the ability to do this since before I even acknowledged Him and now that I'm surrendered, His grace has made my written and spoken words more impactful than I could ever imagine. I'm not the only one. There are tens of thousands of us out there. You might be one of them.

Hallelujah. Him and Him only.

The title is the explanation for this book. It's that simple. Nothing more, nothing less.

How to Consider the Creator in all that you do. Why you should Consider the Creator in all that you do. The impact that Considering the Creator in all that you do will have on your life. The impact that Considering the Creator in all that you do will have on the lives of those you come in contact with.

I took random journal entries, random rebuttals non-believers would say about Christianity and a few random thoughts, then combined them with my life experiences and topped it off with scripture.

I really hope my attempt at being vulnerable ends up being valuable to whoever reads this. Sometimes all it takes to develop more intimacy with the Lord and to get to the next season of your journey is reading a single sentence, a single quote or watching a single scenario play out in someone else's life. This is one of many reasons a Christ centered community is so important.

I'll be adding in (t)asks throughout this book in hopes that you get the full value of these messages. Instead of calling them "tasks", look at them as "asks" that simple perspective change makes a difference.

The scriptures throughout this book are from the English Standard Version (ESV).

If only I would've known God would use all these experiences so that I could gather tools needed for the calling He has placed on my life, my mindset would've been so much different throughout the seasons and I would've surrendered to Him much sooner. Times are dire and the world needs people who will step boldly in the name of Jesus Christ to further advance the kingdom of heaven.

Please don't take as long as I did. Your obedience matters.

Christ is the physical manifestation of God. He is the Son of God. He is the Spotless Lamb. He came to be the example, to testify the truth, to die and resurrect, ultimately defeating death so that those who believe in Him can have eternal life.

CHAPTER 1
THE GOLDEN QUESTION

"Do you believe in God?" I have no clue how many times I've been asked this question. I can't even tell you how many times I've asked myself this question throughout my journey.
There were times in life when I would've given a simple answer to this question without even thinking about it. I would've said "yes" and carried on with the conversation without ever asking myself what it really means to believe in something.
That said, there were times in life when I would've confidently said "no" and would've considered verbally attacking someone for trying to "pry" or "force" God on me. Two completely different answers from the same person… One answer was given during a time of perceived "peace". One answer was given during a time of bitterness and chaos.

The God I speak of, the God I praise, the God I worship is Yahweh, the Triune God, the God of the Israelites, Jehovah Jireh, Elohim, Adonai, Jehovah Rapha, Jehovah Nissi, Jehovah Shalom, Jehovah Raah, Jehovah Shammah, El Elyon, El Olam, Immanuel, El Roi, The mighty God of Jacob, Jehovah Sabaoth, The Father, the Son and the Holy Spirit. I could go on, but you get it… The one and only sovereign God who has reigned from the Heavens since the beginning of time.

Before we can give an honest answer to this question, we must understand what it means to Believe. I think one of the main reasons we have so much conflict in the U.S today, aside from the root of it all, sin, is because we don't have the same understanding of what certain words and phrases mean.

Somehow, we've gotten to a point where some of us think we can recreate everything for our benefit in hopes that there will come a day where nothing in society offends us or makes us question our ideology.

Here are a few simple things to keep in mind.

- Words mean what they mean, not what we make them mean.
- Truth is truth. It can be both refreshing and hurtful.
- Facts are facts, but facts aren't always final.
- Facts change feelings but feelings don't change facts.

(Websters Dictionary 1828) "**BELIE'VE**, *verb* to credit upon the authority or testimony of another; to be persuaded of the truth of something upon the declaration of another, or upon evidence furnished by reasons, arguments, and deductions of the mind, or by other circumstances, than personal knowledge."

(Websters Dictionary 1828) "**TRUTH**, *noun* Conformity to fact or reality; exact accordance with that which is, or has been, or shall be. The *truth* of history constitutes its whole value. We rely on the *truth* of the scriptural prophecies."

(Websters Dictionary 1828) "**FACT**, *noun* Anything done, or that comes to pass; an act; a deed; an effect produced or achieved; an event. Witnesses are introduced into court to prove a *fact* Facts are stubborn things. To deny a *fact* knowingly is to lie."

It seems that not only are we not on the same page with words, but we're also not on the same page with the weight of our words. We go back and forth like a wave in the sea when it comes to our so-called beliefs. We must be careful with the words that come forth from our mouths because they hold weight and every time we find ourselves backtracking on something we once spoke so boldly about; people see our words as less and less valuable, which leads to many internal and external issues in our lives. Scripture warns us of the issues that arise from speaking too soon (to put it in worldly terms).

(ESV) James 3: 5 So also the tongue is a small member, yet it boasts of great things. How great a forest is set ablaze by such a small fire! 6 And the tongue is a fire, a world of unrighteousness. The tongue is set among our members, staining the whole body, setting on fire the entire course of life, and set on fire by hell. 7 For every kind of beast and bird, of reptile and sea creature, can be tamed and has been tamed by mankind, 8 but no human being can tame the tongue. It is a restless evil, full of deadly poison. 9 With it we bless our Lord and Father, and with it we curse people who are made in the likeness of God.

Constantly changing the beliefs we're speaking so boldly about is doing more harm in our lives than good. It's not that we should never admit when our opinions change or

when we're wrong, but opinions, thoughts and beliefs aren't all exactly the same.
It's okay to not have a belief, especially if we don't have the knowledge…

Under the "umbrella" of belief is knowledge. We must be educated on the details of something before we're able to form an actual belief. We can't honestly say that we do believe in something if we aren't truly educated on the details of said thing.

As I mentioned before, there were times when I would answer the golden question with "yes" then I would unapologetically run to drugs, sex, alcohol, people pleasing, violence, or all the above within a short period of time. This would happen often, whether it be during times of stress or times of celebration.
Let me say this in a different way, just to be sure you understand where I was at mentally & spiritually… I would say that I believed in God then I would run to everything that completely opposes & dishonors God.

I replied "yes" to the golden question to acknowledge that a God exists, but I didn't know what this God is called, and I definitely didn't know His word enough to understand what it meant to believe in Him. To be completely honest, I didn't even know enough to confidently say I DIDN'T believe in Him. Saying "no" was my way of "getting back" at God for all the trials I had been through in life. In the back of my mind I hoped that, if God existed, my denial of Him would help me get even with Him. I think many people are carrying this type of bitterness and hatred for God today. It's hard for us to use human logic to make sense of the bad things that have happened to us or the bad things we've seen happen to people we know, so "just in case he is real" people hope to "get back" by denying his existence.

Denying Him doesn't bring peace or understanding of life though. It brings more chaos, confusion, destruction, grief and leads us down a path that only the enemy wants us to go down. No matter what situation you're in, please consider learning about Him. Please consider developing an intimate relationship with Him. Please Consider the Creator.

Matthew 11:28 **Come to me, all who labor and are heavy laden, and I will give you rest.** 29 **Take my yoke upon you, and learn from me, for I am gentle and lowly in heart, and you will find rest for your souls.** 30 **For my yoke is easy, and my burden is light.**

God is everything he says he is. To believe in God you must understand that you're believing in who God says He is, what He says His creation is and how He instructs his creation to live. We must accept all of Him, not just the good, not just what we perceive to be bad, but all of Him. We must come into agreement with Him and His ways instead of coming into agreement with the world. It takes time to learn His word though. Scripture is deep. I think of one of my favorite childhood movies, Shrek, scripture is like an onion, you have to peel it back one layer at a time.

For us to understand the depth of scripture we must seek God in prayer, studying, fasting and meditating on his word, but also remember it takes time, consistent effort and a desire to learn.
It takes the type of time someone puts in to learn an artist's music or an actor's story. It takes the type of time someone puts in to have a solid relationship with a significant other. It takes the type of time it takes someone to be on a first name basis with the bartender. It takes the type of time it takes to learn a professional athlete's stats. It takes intentional time and an understanding that The Bible is not just a regular book with some simple pointers about how to "win" in life.

So, let me ask you… Do you believe in God?

The gate is still narrow.

Spend lots of time processing the reality of this?

CHAPTER 2

GOD DOESN'T SEE PEOPLE HOW PEOPLE SEE PEOPLE

Many Americans live in a constant comparison mindset... or should I dare say, many Americans are bound to coveting and/or idolatry. Everywhere we look, whether it be TV, our phones, tablets, ipads, or billboards we see things we want (material items, physiques, labels). If you're more of a pessimistic person, instead of seeing things you WANT, you see things YOU DON'T HAVE. It's like this every day we wake up. It's so common we don't even notice the world programming us. I initially wanted to say, "that's how it is these days", but in all reality, it's been going on since the garden. Consider Genesis…

Genesis 2:[16] And the Lord God commanded the man, saying, "You may surely eat of every tree of the garden, [17] but of the tree of the knowledge of good and evil you shall not eat, for in the day that you eat of it you shall surely die."

Genesis 3:[3] but God said, 'You shall not eat of the fruit of the tree that is in the midst of the garden, neither shall you touch it, lest you die.'" [4] But the serpent said to the woman, "You will not surely die. [5] For God knows that when you eat of it your eyes will be opened, and you will be like God, knowing good and evil." [6] So when the woman saw that the tree was good for food, and that it was a delight to the eyes, and that the tree was to be desired to make one wise, she took of its fruit and ate, and she also gave some to her husband who was with her, and he ate.

The moment Eve was told she could have something she didn't currently have she was ready to dishonor God, completely turning a blind eye to the repercussions in hopes that she would get "more" out of life. It didn't take much convincing on the serpents part. We always end up desiring what we don't have. We always seem to think we're missing out on something as if God picked everyone in the lineup except for us and then walked away. We always seem to fail at considering the creator and accepting that he has a plan for each and every one of us.

Looking around and seeing things you desire isn't always a bad thing, it's more about where your heart is and whether you're taking that desire to God or not. To a person without faith, it's more than likely going to be a bad thing. To a person without faith, comparison inevitably becomes a lifestyle that, if turned into a reality show, could be titled 'Keeping up With the Jones".

Personally, I would say comparison started influencing me heavily at a young age. I'm biracial (Black & White) and grew up in a predominantly white county… Yes, I said that correctly, not just the town, it was the entire county. I mean, at the time, I was the entire black community.
It didn't take many years of me going to public school to realize I wasn't like the people around me. They were white, I'm biracial. To rural America in the 2000's, I was blackity black, there was no in between.

This area had no shortage of outspoken and simple-minded individuals that didn't know anything other than what pappy taught them and they were willing to die on whatever hill they were raised on. The KKK would actually stand at intersections on occasion and pass out flyers. Yes, they were successfully passing out flyers in the early - mid 2000's. You can google search this to get more details "kkk passing out flyers desloge mo" and "kkk leader leadwood mo".

In addition to being a different color than the people around me, I was the kid that came from a rundown home. Our clothes smelled bad due to lack of cleanliness and our yard was full of trash and stray animals. These circumstances led me to be an angry child, so I was always in confrontations with classmates and to top it off, I didn't care to try in class so I always had bad grades. I remember getting a grade report midway through a semester and I had F's in every class.

In retrospect, it just felt like there was nothing about me that was truly good enough for anything or anyone. Classmates would make hateful comments regularly and I would even hear hateful comments from random people in public, but nothing was as common as the blatant distancing from classmates, a few teachers and parents of classmates.

I did have a few people around who cared about me and showed me love. I was blessed to have them around, but nothing stands out like watching people look at me sideways and distancing themselves all those years. That always seemed to hurt more than any hateful comment.

I'm not saying any of this to have a pity party or to make it seem as if God "dealt me a bad hand".

I'm hoping to paint a picture of how deep-rooted the feeling of inadequacy was within me, so that you can see I'm not shooting in the dark in this chapter. Maybe your struggle wasn't about skin color. Maybe your struggle was about being the "fat kid" or the "adopted kid" or maybe the "weird kid". Regardless, I can relate to the struggles you have dealt with or are dealing with currently. Just to clarify, you may be an adult now, but your mind can still be stuck in the same mode from your childhood, so this is for teenagers and adults. Everything is going to be okay one day.

All the years of feeling like an outsider, I decided to find a way to really fit in as I grew into adolescence. I didn't really excel in the sports I played once I got into high school, so the party scene seemed to be where I would be able to fit in. Not only was it a way for me to fit in, but it was an easy way to blow off some steam that had been building up for as long as I could remember. The rebellion was always in me and it became evident as I got older. To give some insight, I was 12 the first time I got drunk and the first time I got stoned was right after I turned 14.
Getting into the party scene was nothing too crazy to me because I had already dabbled a little. Since the area was far from a big city it was very common for high schoolers to drink and smoke weed because that was the only source

of entertainment for the kids who didn't have much going on in their lives.

House parties were where it was at. The house parties were where the "cool kids" were. Kids from different schools in the area were known for always being at the big parties we called ragers. They were either known for being the life of the party or being the fighter at the party. As a freshman, I was locked in on a goal. I wanted to be one of them one day and it's safe to say I cared about that more than anything. More than sports, more than grades, more than having innocent fun with my friends that had good things going on in their lives.

Well… to make a long story short, I made it. I became the delinquent that all the other partiers knew. I was one of many, but I made it and I soaked up every second of it. This created so many issues in my life that by the time I was able to "wake up" and acknowledge it, many good things had been destroyed.
Often known as a life of the party, once that bottle or can cracked open, I felt like I had to go "Balls to the wall", and I would either end up doing something wild that people loved, I would keep people laughing or, when I needed to blow off extra steam, I would get in a fight (not hard to find in an environment with young hotheads that are drunk and high). Once these things became common I had to up the thrill, so that's when girls in abundance started coming into the picture. Hookup culture is exactly what most young men want to be part of, especially broken young

men that are trying to fill a void without realizing there's a void.

I cannot tell you how many:

- Fights I got into over jealous ex's.
- Pregnancy scares I had.
- STI scares I had.
- Times I regretted who I took home.
- Times I ruined a good relationship.
- Friendships I ruined because it was never actually "bro's before hoes".

*God doesn't tell us about the things we shouldn't do to keep us from enjoying life. He tells us to protect us and the consequences of premarital sex is one of the things he wants to protect us from.

My poor behavior didn't get better after high school, it continued and morphed into something I would've never imagined. By the time I was a few months out of high school, I was getting into popping and snorting pills, heavy drinking, getting high on cough syrup, smoking weed practically all day every day, sniffing cocaine regularly, getting high on air duster (even totaled a car while high on it), continued to "thrive" in hook up culture, and smoked/snorted meth for a season as well.
I was completely lost, and I accepted an extended stay in hell on earth ONLY because I ran to everything but Christ.

All these chaotic and destructive tendencies started piling up in my life because I had to feel validated. That's why it all started. Validation was like a drug. It was like that daily carb heavy snack, great while you're eating it and satisfies you in the moment, but never lasts long, so you'll always need more and you eventually end up regretting it when you look in the mirror to face the reality of where your life has gone.

I thought I was being a "man"... Isn't it ironic that some young men are taught to be "men" by males that are just as damaged as an adult as they were as a teenager? Their bodies developed but their heart & mind never did. My mind goes to Hebrews.

Hebrews 5: [11] About this we have much to say, and it is hard to explain, since you have become dull of hearing. [12] For though by this time you ought to be teachers, you need someone to teach you again the basic principles of the oracles of God. You need milk, not solid food, [13] for everyone who lives on milk is unskilled in the word of righteousness, since he is a child. [14] But solid food is for the mature, for those who have their powers of discernment trained by constant practice to distinguish good from evil.

Grown men, leading young men into a life of chaos, further confirming that misery indeed does love company. Day after day being the God of their own lives, denying the existence of God with their hearts and actions, verbally claiming to believe in God, but never truly considering the creator before speaking, acting, or leading. One of many flaws of the flesh that reveal how truly wretched we are outside of Christ.

This should go without being said; Having sex with random women to feel good about yourself, fighting because you can't control your emotions and getting drunk or high because you want to run from the discomfort of an inevitably difficult life is not what makes a male a man. Being strong spiritually, mentally, morally, handling responsibilities and accepting that it is our call to love as Christ loves are the things that make a male a man.

There were probably 100 different reasons I could've given as to WHY I lived how I did. Ultimately, I ignored the thought of seeking real healing and chose to chase instant gratification, dopamine hits and pats on the back by any means unnecessary. No one will lie to you like you lie to you, and a damaged person will sell themselves on a lie just to find a way to avoid facing the truth about their life circumstances because facing the hurt seems too uncomfortable to bear. All the reasons I could come up with; "I'm young so I'm just having fun" or "you only live once" or "it's normal to be like this" or "I worked a lot this week, so I deserve this", the list goes on. It's all the same things someone who "experiments" with drugs will tell themselves before they become an addict. It's all the things an obese person tells themselves before they eat themselves into heart failure. It's all the things a rebellious kid will tell themselves as they're entering a life of full-blown criminal activity. It's all programmed excuses. Before I get into how this information ties into the title of this chapter, I want to make it clear; God spared me.

God spared a few others I was running with too. I partied and committed crimes with lots of people. Got drunk and high with lots of people that have passed on. Some passed from drug overdose, some died in drinking and driving accidents. Some are currently addicts. Some are still living in a broken-down home with a broken-down heart, wondering why their life is what it is. Some… I have no idea if they're alive or
not. A few are living well, waking up every day and carrying their cross to get closer to the same God you're working to get closer to (you wouldn't be reading this book if you weren't). I was one of the wildest ones in practically every group I was part of. How do the craziest ones steer clear from a life of addiction, incarceration, and death? Looking back, all I can say for sure is God must have a reason to keep His hand on us through all of it.
Before you go on thinking you're too messed up, remember, He doesn't reject those who seek Him no matter what their past is. That's a promise.

GOD DOESN'T SEE PEOPLE HOW PEOPLE SEE PEOPLE.
GOD DOESN'T SEE YOU HOW YOU SEE YOU.
The evidence is all through scripture, so I want to highlight a few verses for you.

Judges 6: 11 Now the angel of the LORD came and sat under the terebinth at Ophrah, which belonged to Joash the Abiezrite, while his son Gideon was beating out wheat in the winepress to hide it from the Midianites. 12 And the angel of the LORD appeared to him and said to him, "The LORD is with you, O mighty man of valor."

***T(ask) Read all of Judges 6.**

Gideon was an Israelite. On more than one occasion the Israelites faced defeat because they always seemed to stray from God. In this story, God handed them over to the Midianites, meaning the midianites happened to find their location and ended up attacking their city, taking control of them. The Midianites were very violent people and would often kill, destroy crops, and take their livestock, leaving the Israelites to starve.

Gideon, being broken down to the point of living in constant fear of the midianites, was approached by an angel of the LORD. He was in a wine press, threshing wheat. For those of you that don't know, wheat was supposed to be threshed on a hilltop. The gusts of wind that came would carry the thresh off into the breeze. A wine press was for making wine. Gideon was doing something in an area he had no business doing it in for the sake of survival.

At this point in time, we could imagine he was so battered and bruised that he forgot about God, living in constant paranoia and feeling defeated. But God.

An angel of the LORD came to let him know that despite all the attacks, God was with him. The little ole, paranoid, battered and beaten Israelite Gideon… God sent a messenger to let him know that he was with him.. If you continue to read, Gideon actually ends up being the one who leads an army to defeat the midianites and ends up bringing his people out of oppression. All by the power of God within him.

Sometimes in life we're Gideon. Beaten up from life with bruises and wounds. Our entire family tree is full of the same pain, abuse, addiction, and depression. That type of history will have us doing things that don't make sense for the sake of survival. We do it because it's learned behavior. We run to alcohol, drugs, sex, greed, suicide attempts, violence, self-loathing etc. because it's what feels good in the moment… It could be because we've forgotten that God has a plan for us. It could be because we've forgotten that God did not give us a spirit of fear but a spirit of peace, love and of a sound mind. It could be because we've forgotten that God is with us always and loves us.

God sent Gideon a messenger to let him know he was with him. When the messenger came he essentially referred to him as a "mighty warrior", even after his people strayed from him and had been plundered by their enemies time and time again.

God didn't create you and send you here to be less than. I'm not saying I know for sure that he sent you here to be wealthy or to always be great at everything you do, but He absolutely has a plan for you that is greater than your human logic could ever fathom. Think about it, the same God that created the sky, warmth from the sun, the oceans, pregnancy, deep breaths, and every ounce of love in life also created you… He felt the need to put you here with all those things, with all these people, and you were necessary to be here at this time.

You're a masterpiece, regardless of how you feel about yourself and regardless of what people say about you. You may need some work, but beneath all of that, you're nothing less than a masterpiece crafted by THE Creator of creators.
Notice that the angel coming to Gideon and calling him a "man of valor" happened before he was known to be a hero or warrior. Notice that God picked Gideon before he knew he was capable of such a thing. You don't have to be famous. You don't have to be wealthy. You don't need to have anything other than faith and a desire to be obedient to carry out what God calls you to do.

Anointing of David
T(ask) Start in 1 Samuel 16

David was a Shepheard and considered the weakest of his family. He had 7 brothers; some were warriors that fought in the Israelite army with King Saul. Samuel was instructed by God to find the new king in Bethlehem at Jesse's home (David's father).
When Samuel arrived at the home Jesse presented 7 sons to Samuel in hopes that one of them would be chosen by God to be king over Israel. Samuel sees the first son, Eliab, he thought he would be the one God would choose because of his stature and the fact that he was a seasoned

warrior. God speaks to Samuel upon approaching Eliab, which can be found in 1 Samuel.

1 Samuel 16: 7 But the LORD said to Samuel, "Do not look on his appearance or on the height of his stature, because I have rejected him. For the LORD sees not as man sees: man looks on the outward appearance, but the LORD looks on the heart."

Samuel asked for confirmation from God after seeing the 7 sons, but God didn't choose any of them. Then Samuel asked Jesse if he had any other sons, as he was certain God had sent him to the right place. Jesse said he had one more son, but he tended the sheep. This shows us that Jesse didn't think he was an option to be a king because he was basically a runt in their eyes. When Samuel met David, God let Samuel know that David was to be the future king of Israel.

David didn't leave home and become king right away, there were many twists and turns in his journey, but just think about the anointing portion of the story for a minute. David's family didn't even mention him until they had to. Even when his father, Jesse, told Samuel about him he made sure to mention that he was just a "Shepheard". His own father didn't see anything special in him, neither did any of his 7 brothers. The people closest to him, the people that knew everything about him, had no idea what lived within him. God has the final say. Only the creator knows what the creation is made for.

Consider the Creator before coming into agreement with what others say about you.
Consider the Creator before assuming your worth to the world.
The key to finding out is to get close with God (consecrate) and do everything with God in mind.
That's how David killed Goliath... He did it for God and with God.
That's how David ruled as king and was successful in years of battle... he did it for God and with God.

What would you be capable of doing if you did it for God and with God?
What would you be capable of if you were to come out of agreement with the ways of the world and come into agreement with the Kingdom of Heaven?

Someone cannot give you what they don't have. Instead of taking your frustration out on them, take it to God.

CHAPTER 3

"IF HE WERE REAL, HE WOULDN'T LET THAT HAPPEN"

You've probably heard this many times. You may have been the one to say this at times. I've heard it said and I've been the person saying it, which is why I believe I can confidently provide a reasonable response to this statement.

Response: I'm sure what you're going through is tough. You may feel alone and you may not understand the reason for this life or the things that happen in it. We must remember that, as humans who basically just arrived on earth, we don't have a full understanding of how God works. We weren't here when He laid the foundation of the earth so we don't understand His plan, we just know He has one and we have to trust Him. He is on the throne. No one is moving Him. You can trust Him.
When someone doesn't read scripture they have this misunderstanding of how God works. They think God will only allow "good" things to happen to keep us from being uncomfortable in life. Why do we try to make the rules for what's good and what's bad? This idea only confirms that we are truly like children to God. He has existed forever and here we are trying to make the rules for life after only being here for a few years. That's like a toddler trying to argue with an adult about something the adult has had knowledge on for 30 years… we are the toddler.

Anytime someone mentions a good thing or a bad thing, a good person or a bad person, I can't help but to think "good or bad based on whose standard?"... I can't help but to consider the creator.
Looking back on Christ' life, we see Him being tempted by the enemy, ridiculed by non-believers, abandoned by His disciples, we even see Him beaten beyond the point of recognition and crucified. Jesus was the only perfect person that has ever walked the face of the earth and He still suffered. Additionally, we have to remember that God NEVER once told us life would or should be easy. He actually says quite the opposite. We see suffering in practically every story in scripture. Suffering has been part of God's refining process since the beginning.

*T(ask)
Read Genesis 2-3
Genesis 2-3 will give you the answer to WHY bad things happen. You'll get the answer directly from scripture.

Death was near me for as long as I can remember. One of my earliest memories was being held by my grandpa at the funeral of a loved one. I didn't know what was going on at the moment, but I do remember being so little that he was holding me while he conversed with family. I've been to so many funerals I still can't stand the smell of flowers. I still struggle to understand the point of giving flowers to someone grieving the loss of a loved one "here you go, watch these die too".

The first tough loss I took was when I was 11. My grandpa lost his battle with lung cancer. He was my first best friend, my first father figure and my first role model growing up. I didn't have the best relationship with my grandmother, so I always felt like my grandpa was all I ever had. Yes, I had a few friends at school, family members I would see, and I had two siblings in the household at the time, but my grandpa was everything to me. He taught me how to work on things, taught me how important a good work ethic is, taught me about the outdoors and showed me how to be tough. The men understand the importance of a role model instilling toughness in them as a young boy.
After he passed, there were many, many days when I didn't want to be alive anymore. When we would drive past the cemetery I would look the other way (this went on for a few years).
When I was around family, whether it be immediate or distant, and they wanted to talk about him I couldn't take it. If they wanted to stop at the cemetery to clean his headstone or reminisce, I would sit in the car and cry. Man... that hurt bad, and it hurt for a long time.

There were other things going on in my life before this happened though. My mother wasn't around much, I didn't know my biological father, we lived in a filthy, dingy singlewide trailer, I was the only student at my school that wasn't white, and my grandmother seemed to dislike me (she had her own issues). There were just lots of things that made me feel like I was never enough, it felt like life would never be good for me.

As any child, I had my good days, but reality would be sure to slap me in the face if I ever forgot where I came from or what I looked like. This constant reminder of my reality eventually drove me to a suicide attempt when I was 12. Yes, I attempted suicide before entering my teenage years and it wasn't a "cry for attention", it was a full-blown attempt. I thought of a few different ways to do it, but I guess a process of elimination led me to either hanging myself or bleeding out. There wasn't anything in my room high enough to hang myself from and I knew if I could reach the ground I wouldn't follow through with it, so that left me with the latter. I ended up smashing a soda can and ripping it in half. I used the sharp edge of it to cut myself. The idea was to bleed out before anyone could stop it from happening, so I sawed away at the top of my hand for several minutes, not realizing that I would've had a better chance cutting on a different area. Every spot I tried would bleed, but I couldn't get deep enough to open the vein. I eventually wiped the blood off with a shirt and carried on with my sulking. I'll never forget the feeling of it though. Not only was it extremely painful, but the adrenaline rush I got while sawing on my skin was like something I had never felt. I was shaking uncontrollably. My heart was racing. My thoughts were all over the place. My skin was screaming.

When I think back to it, I'm not sure if it was impossible to do with the object I was using or If God just wouldn't allow it to happen. Either way, words cannot describe how thankful I am that I wasn't successful at it.

I was so deep in the darkness that I forgot about the good things in life, which is very easy to do when you're secluded and in a depressive state. 1 Peter tells us to be alert and sober minded because the enemy prowls around like a roaring lion looking for something to devour. I believe this applies to drugs and alcohol, but I also believe it applies to emotions that lead to detrimental states of mind. Depression is not a sober mind. Lust is not a sober mind. Anger usually isn't a sober mind. Greed is not a sober mind.

1 Peter 5:8 Be sober-minded; be watchful. Your adversary the devil prowls around like a roaring lion, seeking someone to devour.

This was the first big hit I took in life, but more came after it. We had a close family friend my sisters and I called "Uncle Mike". He was another type of father figure. He lived right up the road from us so we spent lots of time with him over the years.
One night my grandma woke me up and said Uncle Mike had to be taken to the hospital in an ambulance. We all got dressed, got in the car, and left for the hospital, which was only about 15 minutes away. We ended up getting halfway there before my grandma got a call. Uncle Mike died. I was numb by this point, but I remember being really confused. It almost felt like someone was trying to pull a sick prank on me. My grandpa died October 13th, 2005, then Uncle Mike died December 18th, 2006. It truly felt like my life was a bad dream and continued to feel like it throughout my teenage years. Therapy wasn't a thing that anyone around

me would've suggested at the time, we all just "toughed it out". We toughed everything out.
Let me tell you something that I wish I would've known. The weight that comes with some of life's toughest circumstances is entirely too heavy to carry alone and builds pressure at such a rate that bottling it all up can only last for a short period of time. There will eventually be a straw that breaks the camel's back and nothing but chaos will come from it.

Those two losses hit hard, but the hardest one was when I was 21. My aunt and uncle took custody of me right after I turned 13. My aunt was my 2nd mother figure and my uncle was my 3rd father figure. I wanted to move in with them for years because of the tough relationship I had with my grandma, and it only got worse after my grandpa passed. A couple years after losing my grandpa, my grandma finally agreed to let me go live with them. I think the loss led her to the conclusion that I would be better off in a different environment and I think she needed to learn how to live life without him being next to her. It was probably the best move for the both of us.

I remember my aunt called the landline to let me know she was on the way to pick me up. It was a big day for me. It felt like I had hit the lottery and was packing my bags to get out of the ghetto forever. I couldn't leave that place fast enough. My aunt and uncle picked me up, we got dinner at a local steakhouse then they took me shopping to buy clothes because all I had when they came to get me was a trash bag almost all the way full. They treated me like their own child. They're part of the small group of people who truly gave me unconditional love. I lived with them permanently for the next 5 years. As many teenagers, I had the idea I was going to be "free" after I turned 18, so I moved out right after I graduated high school but due to my crazy lifestyle I ended up living there off and on for the next 3 years.

In September of 2016 my aunt and uncle went on vacation with two of their biological children (my 2 little cousins). It was a big deal for them because my uncle had started a business years prior and worked relentlessly to build it for quite a while. They eventually worked into a position of being able to comfortably afford taking a vacation to Disney world.
After several days of visiting Disney they left to see Daytona beach because it was a bucket list destination for my uncle. On their way to Daytona they were sideswiped by another vehicle and lost control, crashing into a tree off the side of the highway.

That was the worst phone call I've ever picked up. I remember I just ate lunch, chicken breast and whole green beans. I was sitting in the recliner to relax before I went into work for the evening and suddenly had a strong urge to call my grandma, but my phone started ringing as soon as I had the thought. It was my sister, Samantha, and she was hysterical, which instantly made me sick to my stomach. I answered "hello" after a few moments of silence she responded "Aunt Sarah and Uncle Greg got in a wreck". Hoping that if anyone was hurt it would be minor injuries at most. I said "ok, is everyone alright?" The silence felt like it lasted an hour. She responded with a shaky voice "No. They died"... There aren't words to explain the feeling that came over me at that moment. It's not an emotion that can be manufactured and it's definitely not something you forget. It's such an overload of emotions exploding within your being that you can't process even a fraction of what's going on. It paralyzes you.

I kept thinking "This isn't real. There's no way this really happened" then a few seconds later the repetitive thought was "Why? Why? Why?". These were my subconscious thoughts for weeks. Not just one, but two of the people who raised me, two of the people who saved my life, just died at the same time. No warning. Just gone.

My little cousins survived, but were airlifted to Arnold Palmer Hospital in Orlando, where they stayed in the ICU for a while. They eventually made a full physical recovery. The road to recovery for all of us was a very dark and emotional one. The matriarch and patriarch of the family were gone, which led to quite a bit of dysfunction and became more extreme as time went on. It was a terrible season, but we eventually made it through.

Needless to say, this combination of circumstances made it easy for me to think things like "if God was real that wouldn't have happened" or "if God were real, bad things wouldn't happen to me". That was my mindset throughout most of my life. Even when I would visit a church in hopes of finding some type of comfort, as much as I wanted to believe in God, I would always be reminded of the past. I couldn't make sense of WHY these things would happen to ME. Not being able to figure it out had a huge impact on my subconscious and perspective on life.

I've found there are many verses that help during tough times like the ones I mentioned, but there's one chapter in particular that hit me deep in my spirit. Job 38.

Job 38 Then the LORD answered Job out of the whirlwind and said: [2]
"Who is this that darkens counsel by words without knowledge?
[3] Dress for action like a man; I will question you, and you make it
known to me. [4] "Where were you when I laid the foundation of the
earth? Tell me, if you have understanding. 5 Who determined its
measurements—surely you know!
Or who stretched the line upon it? 6 On what were its bases sunk,
or who laid its cornerstone, 7 when the morning stars sang together
and all the sons of God shouted for joy? 8 "Or who shut in the sea
with doors
when it burst out from the womb, 9 when I made clouds its garment
and thick darkness its swaddling band, 10 and prescribed limits for it
and set bars and doors, 11 and said, 'Thus far shall you come, and no
farther,
and here shall your proud waves be stayed'?

Scripture tells us Job was a faithful man, blameless and upright. He faced terrible trials in life that most of us couldn't imagine going through. Job basically asks God why he was facing so many trials, as he was a man of faith that didn't deserve anything bad to happen to him by human standards. "Where were you when I laid the foundation of the earth?" Woah. That instantly made me want to sit down and never speak another word.

Really think about it.. where were YOU when the earth's foundation was laid? We have no clue. We don't know how it happened, what it sounded like, what it looked like, when it happened, why it happened… Therefore, we have no clue what His full plan is for us. Nowadays, I'm completely content with God doing whatever He wants to do because I'm thankful I don't have to handle even a fraction of the responsibilities He handles. I'm thankful that He does have a plan for me that will be far beyond anything I could ever dream up for myself. We truly have every reason to trust Him, as he's been very clear, consistent and sure to set us up for success in this life.

We can't possibly make sense of why God allows certain things to happen. When I think about death, abandonment, and all the other uncomfortable things that happened in my life I realize I wasn't the only person who experienced those things. I realized there aren't any situations I can be in that someone else hasn't already made it through by the power of God. I realized the end of someone else's life had nothing to do with me, their life ended because God allowed it to end, for a rhyme or reason that I can't possibly understand. Their death had an impact on me, but it wasn't an attack on me.

God has a very interesting way of making sure the misfortunes don't go to waste. God uses everything.

He uses absolutely everything for good at some point in time. He doesn't do things without reason, he's too intentional for that.

Romans 8: 28 And we know that for those who love God all things work together for good, for those who are called according to his purpose.

You may be asking yourself "how can someone passing away be used for good?"
Reflecting on the time spent with loved ones and the quickness of their life ending helped me be a better person. Loss led me to appreciate people more. Loss led me to look for the good within people even if they didn't see it themselves.
Although my loved ones were gone and in a different realm that I will never be able to see on this side of life, there came a time when my poor decision making didn't sit right with me because it could've made them look like bad parents. This mindset shift took time though, it was far from an overnight change. It took lots of reflection and contemplation.
When death hits close to you, it's natural to start evaluating your life. You start to ask yourself questions you've never thought of before... What's important to me? Not what society says I should care about, but what means the most to me in life?
If I were to die right now, what have I done that truly mattered in a positive way?

If I were to die right now, how would the people in my life feel about the relationship we had?
What would God say to me about how I lived if I died right now?

As far as the positives that come with understanding depression, suicide and feeling inadequate, I think about relatability. Those things added value to your testimony so you can relate to the people you were sent here to help. When tragedy strikes, you'll either spend the rest of your life sulking or you'll learn to pull the positives. You may not see positives in the moment, but at some point down the road the positives come to the surface, especially if you ask God to reveal them to you.

Remember that He has a plan for you and it entails many things you don't know about yet. Your life experiences are the puzzle pieces that eventually come together to create the bigger picture. Not every piece is pretty and vibrant, some are dark and shaped in such a weird way that you have no clue where they would fit in.
Remember, you're here for a legitimate reason. Trust in Him with all your heart and do not lean on your own understanding.
Remember, you're not the circumstance, you're just going through the circumstance. Remember, you must pull the positives. They're there, you just have to be willing to see them.

I don't believe the worst "generational curses" are alcoholism, addiction or poverty. I believe the worst "generational curse" is pride, and it's been taking entire bloodlines out since the beginning of time.

CHAPTER 4

God's Timing

Ecclesiastes 3:1-8

3 For everything there is a season, and a time for every matter under heaven:

2 a time to be born, and a time to die;
a time to plant, and a time to pluck up what is planted;
3 a time to kill, and a time to heal;
a time to break down, and a time to build up;
4 a time to weep, and a time to laugh;
a time to mourn, and a time to dance;
5 a time to cast away stones, and a time to gather stones together;
a time to embrace, and a time to refrain from embracing;
6 a time to seek, and a time to lose;
a time to keep, and a time to cast away;
7 a time to tear, and a time to sew;
a time to keep silence, and a time to speak;
8 a time to love, and a time to hate;
a time for war, and a time for peace.

One of the hardest things to understand in life, the perfection of God's timing. In today's world almost everything is close to instant. If we're cold, we push a button or turn a knob and the temperature of the room changes. If we're bored we pick something that will occupy us for a short period of time, the options to choose from are endless, phone, tv, gaming console, iPad, tablet, headphones, computers, etc.

If we want to go somewhere we hop in a car, probably a push to start, and drive it wherever we want. If we want to see someone, we can facetime, skype, or zoom with them in an instant. If we're feeling tired throughout the day we can use caffeine to get us energized, which typically kicks in within 30 minutes.

If we can't sleep, we can take a sleeping aid, which also typically kicks in within 30 minutes.
I could go on and on about how good we have it when it comes to making sure we have the things we want and having them in a timely manner. The point is, we've gotten so accustomed to things being instant that we've become very impatient and impatient is the opposite of what we need to be if we want to live a successful life by God's standard.

A few important things to know about time:

1. We don't get it back.
2. It goes by regardless of how you feel.
3. It won't stop for you to take a break.
4. God created time, so we have to trust him with it.

I wanted to be important to the world all my life. I wanted people to respect me and look up to me as a role model. When I was a kid I would sit outside in rural Missouri while the crickets and frogs sang their nighttime melodies and daydream about being on a big platform one day. I would imagine myself speaking in front of thousands of people who wanted to listen to what I had to say. Out of all the times I thought about it, I never considered what it would take for me to get to the "big stage". It seemed like if I did something cool a few times, like partied hard enough or made music about the "luxurious life", I would make it there and know exactly how to handle it. It's illogical to think things can be handed to us without going through a season of being equipped. This may be a common denominator when it comes to some failed businesses and ministries… blindness to the lack of proper equipment.

Personally, I couldn't be more thankful that this "breakthrough" didn't happen when I wanted or how I wanted it to happen. If God would've allowed me to be on a large platform promoting the life I was living as a young adult there would have been thousands of people to follow my lead. Who knows how many people I would've influenced to go down a dark path of self destruction. Not only would I have been a bad influence, but I would've handled every opportunity wrong. I had no financial education or discipline, no emotional discipline, no sexual discipline, no care to be of sober mind, and I was easily influenced by reckless people older than me. If I were put on a large platform at a young age I would've self-destructed in no time.

In retrospect it's easy to see I needed to live more life and experience more things in order for my character to develop. My emotional maturity, moral compass, ability to make good decisions, faith and ability to say "no" to the things everyone else was saying "yes" to all needed serious development. God knew long before I did. Praise be to Him for keeping me from my desires. Most of the time it's not external sources that are our biggest threat, it's the chaos going on inside of us that's usually the biggest threat in our life.

We see this inner chaos manifest with celebrities all the time. Whether it be young athletes, influencers, actors, music artists, CEO's and executives. We've seen them go to prison, catch drug charges, illegal gun charges, domestic violence charges, struggle with addiction, file for bankruptcy, lose custody of their children and all kinds of other things. Many times, when someone gets in a high position and/or reaches the status of wealth before their character is developed their life completely spirals out of control. Humans weren't built to bear the weight of the internal and external issues that come with such a thing on their own, it takes divine intervention for us to live at that level successfully. Without that divine intervention, life will eventually derail and we'll undoubtedly mislead people who are following us along the way.
Be thankful for the time your process takes. God knows what you're doing. He knows the twists and turns of the journey you're on. He knows the internal and external threats that are waiting around the corner. Invite Him in. He wants to be involved in everything you do because he knows you won't truly be successful long term without Him. When you think about all the different avenues in which we can take to develop intimacy with Him (prayer, scripture, fellowship, worship, biblical fasting etc.) you come to realize that He has given us all what we need in order to do so, we just have to surrender daily and invite Him in.

Is He preparing you or is He protecting you from something you think you need?

Is it in His will for you to do what you have planned or is it contrary to His will for your life?

The only way you can know for sure is to surrender and seek intimacy with him.
When we think about stories in the Old Testament, the life of Christ and how the Holy Spirit prompts us at certain times it becomes very clear that timing is of the utmost importance in relation to carrying out the will of God. This is completely contrary to human nature due to our innate lack of understanding as well as how our minds have been programmed by the ways of the world. I always imagine how happy satan must be knowing how short our attention spans are and how impatient we are. Many people would rather act impulsively a hundred times then deal with the consequences later on than to wait for God and only have to move once. If I could speak purely by speculation, I would say satan is very much at work and is more successful at reprogramming our minds than we would like to give him credit for. See, if he can get us to move throughout life without considering God or only thinking about God after our impulsive decisions have gotten us in a bad spot, he can get us to spend this ONE life walking everywhere but in the calling that has been

placed on it by God. Steal, kill and destroy. We don't think deep enough about the means by which he will take in order to make this happen. He wants to steal our joy, our purpose, our hope, our desire to seek intimacy with God and our faith that God truly does love us and wants us to have life abundantly. He wants to kill us and everyone we love because God created us. He wants to destroy every dream, every relationship, every career, everything and everyone that leads people to Christ. He can do all of these things by setting the world systems up to be fast paced and over stimulating because he knows distraction is an enemy of God's direction.

I think we would all be smart to be intentional about taking our impatience to God in prayer every day. God created us and He created time, so only he knows how we, as humans, can truly couple with time in order to move according to his plan. I also think we would be smart to be intentional about doing things that train us to develop patience. Start doing things like sitting in silence by yourself, watching longer form educational content instead of living on short form social media platforms, wake up earlier than normal so you can have a slow and peaceful morning before the chaos starts, start playing checkers or chess. Those are a few examples of easy things you can do on your part to become more patient, but just know, when you ask for it, God will give you situations that lead you to exercise your ability or inability to be patient. Our level of patience and ability to wait for God to reveal his orchestration for our life will show how steadfast our faith truly is. We all fall into fear of being "behind", anxiousness that comes from fear, and so on, but try to keep in mind that His plan is so much better than any plan we could ever come up with. Do your best to recall what you've read about in scripture. Remember that He never fails and He always comes through for those who endure patiently. Here are a few scriptures to meditate on. Hopefully diving into these will ease your mind and encourage you to seek understanding of what God is doing in your life right now so that you get the things you need for what he has planned for your future.

Ephesians 5:15-16

15 Look carefully then how you walk, not as unwise but as wise, 16 making the best use of the time, because the days are evil.

Daniel 2:21

21 He changes times and seasons;
he removes kings and sets up kings;
he gives wisdom to the wise
and knowledge to those who have understanding;

Galatians 4:4

2 but he is under guardians and managers until the date set by his father. 3 In the same way we also, when we were children, were enslaved to the elementary principles of the world. 4 But when the fullness of time had come, God sent forth his Son, born of woman, born under the law, 5 to redeem those who were under the law, so that we might receive adoption as sons. 6 And because you are sons, God has sent the Spirit of his Son into our hearts, crying, "Abba! Father!" 7 So you are no longer a slave, but a son, and if a son, then an heir through God.

Conviction is not condemnation. Conviction is a grace. Accept it while you can.

CHAPTER 5

All it took was a conversation

Journal entry: THE MOTHER GOD GAVE ME.

"God put me in an interesting family situation, as he did many people. I spent many years of my childhood hoping that my mom would be able to take custody of me and my sister. I had assumed that if it happened, my life would be a "normal life" like everyone else… that never happened. I spent many years confused as to why she was how she was, why she acted like she was thriving in life but her circumstances never showed it, why she bragged about having wealthy friends and traveling the world but didn't come to visit me and Samantha much. "Why?" seemed to be a question that crossed my mind a lot. When I came to Christ my questions were answered. "She's a human being". At the foundational level of life, she's not a mom or a daughter or a sister.. She's a human. The combination of her decisions + uncontrollable life circumstances = she was brutally assaulted by life. She had to survive and one of the ways to do it was to always run from reality, to always tell herself and others that life was better than it really is. I hope I'm able to pay for her housing one day, I hope I'm able to get her eating healthy and pay for her therapy. She needs help, as we all need help. Sometimes she really gets on my nerves. For some reason, I feel like no one gets on my nerves as quick as she can,

which is mostly my fault. She is how she is just as I am how I am. I took a trip to see her in Chicago this weekend. I'm not sure what triggered it, but I suddenly realized how much I love her. She's such a loving, compassionate and thoughtful person. I spent so much time being frustrated with her that I haven't looked her in the eyes much and I came to this realization as I was leaving Chicago. Hopefully we have many more years to live together. Hopefully my kids (God willing) will get to spend lots of quality time with her. That being said, I asked myself what I would regret if I were to leave Chicago and never see her again… all I could think of is I would wish I looked her in the eyes more.
I love my mom with all my heart. "

This is the exact journal entry I wrote that morning. The entire chapter won't be about my mother, but this journal entry sparked many thoughts about perspective and forgiveness that I want to expand on.
To remind you of my family dynamic growing up, my sister and I didn't know our biological fathers, we didn't get to see our mother much at all and we were adopted by our grandparents.
The relationship with my mother was good throughout my childhood. We spoke on the phone fairly often and saw each other once a year on average. I was used to it, so I never really put much thought into it until I was a teenager. Once I grew into adulthood and started connecting dots

from my perspective, I started to hold quite a bit of resentment toward her for several reasons. We eventually had a fall out when I was 25. We didn't speak for nearly 2 years.

One night when I didn't have anything going on I decided to take a drive through the city by myself. That was something I always liked to do back when I smoked. I would listen to music, light one up and drive around the city to see all the lights. Early in the drive that night I got the urge to call my mom. This urge was a little different to me because when the thought crossed my mind I held no resentment toward her and I didn't dread the idea of using "me time" to spend an unknown amount of time talking to her on the phone. This call ended up being 3 hours long. It seemed like we talked about everything. I got everything off my chest, which I had never done before. She was honest and transparent with me about many personal things, which had never happened before. By the time the call was over it felt like I had forgiven her for everything. I failed to realize how heavy the resentment I held toward her was, but God made sure I felt the relief after having the conversation with her that night. We've had our disagreements, as any parent and child would have, but we've been on good terms since this conversation. That's all it took to get to a point of forgiveness so that the relationship could be rebuilt, a conversation.

Many believers have crazy stories about how they were saved. I don't have a particular experience that stands out, but I do have a few that let me know the Holy Spirit had indwelled me and was sanctifying me. The same random urge to contact someone close to me that I had fallen out with happened several times throughout that year. It happened with someone who was one of my best friends for years, we were so close everyone thought we were brothers. We hadn't spoken for a year and a half, but God. God did the same exact, sporadic thing to mend that relationship.

One morning I was sitting on my couch watching a sermon. Unfortunately, I don't remember exactly what the pastor said that sparked this chain of events, but it was something along the lines of forgiveness. While I was watching, one of my old friends came to mind and for the first time in over a year I could think about him without feeling any bitterness toward him. I've always been a bit of a sporadic decision maker, but when I surrendered to Christ that sporadic side of me only increased. I called the old friend to tell him what had just happened in my mind while I was watching the sermon and the next thing I knew, we had set up a time to meet. We met, got things off our chest, caught up and the rest is history. We aren't best friends like we used to be, but we're on good terms. No longer carrying the burden of bitterness toward him is what I needed and God knew it. I realized that most platonic relationships end due to a simple misunderstanding that isn't communicated. If things aren't communicated, neither person has understanding and without understanding, assumptions are made. A house divided cannot stand.

It also happened with one of my grandmothers. We didn't speak for nearly 2 years. This one was a little more dramatic than a phone call though. God put it on my heart to book a flight to visit her and my grandpa one random summer and He didn't let me forget about His presence throughout the entire trip. It seemed like everywhere I went in public He revealed himself through people, even the uber driver I booked once I landed in Houston. It was an hour drive from the airport to my grandparents' place and we conversed about God most of that trip. I couldn't help but to spend that entire trip considering the creator. Looking back, I think He wanted me to remember Him throughout the trip because it was a little nerve racking for me. Randomly flying 900 miles away to have uncomfortable conversations I had been avoiding for nearly 2 years had me second guessing all of it even as I was getting on the plane. He wanted me to remember it was Him that put it on my heart to do so, it wasn't ME, and because it was Him who orchestrated this, everything that was supposed to happen would happen. He wanted me to rest in knowing it was His plan.

I'll never forget the moment I arrived in their driveway.. We pulled up in front of their place and it was like a movie scene. My grandma was outside watering the grass. She had a sunhat and shades on to protect her from the scorching summer TX sun. As I got out she stared at me, trying to figure out whose car was pulling up and who showed up to her home unannounced. When she realized it was me she couldn't believe it. She dropped the sprayer right where she stood and walked over to me. We hugged

for what felt like an hour then we went inside so she could tell my grandpa. It was one of the most beautiful things I've ever experienced in life. They still talk about it today as if it's one of their life highlights. We have the ability to create beautiful moments in our loved ones' lives that they'll never forget when we put our pride to the side and lean on God. All it took was a conversation and I've been on good terms with them since.
2 years of no communication simply because of a disagreement where everyone's feelings were hurt. 2 years?

Not only did God lead me through these situations, but He also revealed the destruction of pride to me. Pride is good for no one. I know there are people out there that say pride is good for things like knowing your value or being aware of what you bring to the table, but I don't believe pride and ego are the right words for what some of those people are trying to say. Pride is absolutely destructive. It is a tool of the enemy that divides and destroys. As much as my flesh wants to take credit for all the "self-help" things I tried over the years to find a sense of peace, I can't. Like I mentioned, I spent lots of time trying to process the things that had happened between myself and the people I mentioned, but God got ahold of my heart and practically softened it within an instant. Jehovah Rapha, Lord who heals.
I've come to realize this is something only God can do. It happens by the power of the Holy Spirit within the believer.

Yes, you can use your own strength to swallow your pride enough to "make amends" with someone you've had a rough past with, but the bitterness will still linger. It may not manifest itself in the way you've always thought when you think about bitterness, but it will manifest and it will likely be very subtle. It shows itself in ways like making plans with someone who offended you in the past, then canceling because you've convinced yourself they don't deserve your time whenever they want to have it. It shows itself within the lack of reassurance you give a supposed friend who hurt you when they vent to you about things because you feel they left you out to dry, so you need to make sure they get a small dose of what you felt. It's all those little things that expose our heart and show us how much we fall short at loving people as Christ loved. God can remove the bitterness and everything that comes with it if you would take it to him. I've experienced this first hand, on many occasions, so I hope you take your relationships to him so you can live in the same freedom. These experiences were much needed, but I didn't know how necessary they were while I was caught up in the emotions of what had happened. I had no clue the weight I was carrying by not being able to forgive. I had no clue the weight that came with my refusal to acknowledge where my faults were in those relationships. Pride wouldn't allow me to admit I was hurt. Pride never allowed me to see that I needed to forgive, it didn't allow me to see those individuals had their own perspective of the situation that they valued more than mine, just as I valued my perspective more than theirs.

With all the loss I experienced in the past you would think I could've understood the importance of spending time with loved ones and making the most of that time, but pride. The flesh is too flawed. Pride is too destructive. The enemy is too crafty. I'm telling you now, you do not want to lose someone close to your heart while being on bad terms with them or knowing you never showed them how much you love and appreciate them. It's a regret that lingers much longer than you could ever imagine, and you may have been able to avoid it through praying for your ability to forgive and courage to be vulnerable. I know those two words are scary, but God will help you with it if you ask Him.

I want to be very clear about this. I'm not encouraging anyone to rekindle a toxic relationship with their ex and I'm not saying that just because you have a conversation with someone everything will be perfect and the two of you will skip off into a field of roses. All relationships take work. They take communication, transparency, grace and understanding, not just one time, but every day. You have to be intentional. You have to accept that there will be uncomfortable conversations, and you cannot expect people to think how you think or handle situations how you handle situations. Seek God in this. Ask Him to give you a heart to love as Christ loves, eyes to see people how He sees people and the desire to forgive as He forgives.

Ask the Holy Spirit to give you discernment so you can navigate these tough conversations. You cannot successfully do it on your own, our flesh is too flawed to do so.

What relationship(s) need healing?
Where did you go wrong?
What are your character flaws that led to the fall out?
What do you want to say and what is the best way to say it?
Would having a conversation help them heal as well?

Be encouraged by knowing this is what God wants for his people, so when you step away from this book and the emotions aren't as strong, remember that how you felt when reading this and thinking about what relationship(s) need healing, is real. In person is always the better route if it's possible. I strongly encourage you to make this a priority.

If you study God's word and find yourself disagreeing, just know you're either not understanding or you're wrong.

CHAPTER 6

Consecration

To some of you reading this, consecration is a new term. It definitely hasn't been common to hear in the circles of believers I've been around over the years, which is a bit alarming, although not using the term doesn't necessarily mean one doesn't live a consecrated life. I have a friend that leads a Bible study at our church every other week. In one study he mentioned the word "consecration" and referred to it as a "Christianese" type word. He's 100% right in saying that, but the more I thought about it, the more it bothered me, not what he said, but the fact that we know it's not a common term used when it comes to faith. This may be the hardest chapter for me to write because I want to tell the truth without giving too much of my opinion, but also without coming across as legalistic. I'll have to refrain from going off on a hundred different tangents because there are so many more things I could say in addition to the main points.

I think there's lots of confusion nowadays when it comes to anything Christianity and ONE of the biggest contributors to that is people speaking "authoritatively" on something when it's really 100% their opinion. We have to walk with a level of humility that allows us to clarify "this is what I THINK when it comes to ____" or "based on my biblical knowledge this is what I believe ____" or "I'm not saying this is law". Christianity isn't about getting viral podcast clips to show the world you found groundbreaking information that no one has ever heard in thousands of years. Is it possible? Yes, but let's not make perceived knowledge an idol and let's not allow pride to be the driver of our tongue.

Yes, there are some things, essentials if you will, that are solidified and can be spoken about confidently. Things like God being triune (God the father, God the son, God the Holy Spirit), Christ is the physical manifestation of God and came to be the example, to testify the truth and to die so that we may be forgiven for our sins if we believe in him. We should all be on the same page with these things, even if you would phrase it a little differently than I do.

(Webster Dictionary 1828) **CONSECRATE**, "*verb* To make or declare to be sacred, by certain ceremonies or rites; to appropriate to sacred uses; to set apart, dedicate, or devote, to the service and worship of God; as, to *consecrate* a church."

"To set apart" meaning, to be set apart from the ways of the world. What are the ways of the world?

1 John 2: [15] Do not love the world or the things in the world. If anyone loves the world, the love of the Father is not in him. [16] For all that is in the world—the desires of the flesh and the desires of the eyes and pride of life—is not from the Father but is from the world. [17] And the world is passing away along with its desires, but whoever does the will of God abides forever.

For the sake of understanding the opposite of consecration, let's flesh out this portion of scripture just to give you some ideas of what these three worldly ways look like in modern times.

Desires of the flesh: Trying to satisfy an endless void in your heart with temporary satisfaction. Continuing to try, but always feeling empty in the end. Sexual immorality, Weed, Drugs, Alcohol, gluttony, greed. These are the things I was running to before Christ, and they never helped, it was like putting a band aid on a wound that needed 100 stitches. What would that be like? A band aid on a gash that large.. The bleeding may stop for a split second, but it will surely start gushing again. If you continue treating the wound with a band aid an infection will set in and the problem will spread, just like sin spreads and slowly eats away at your life. Similarly, running to those things ended up making my life worse because the enemy loves to influence an intoxicated mind. People think the enemy only works how Hollywood has shown us, a head spins around 360 degrees, someone starts bleeding out of their eyes or they grow horns on their head. Lowkey, I wish it was that obvious, but most of the time it's not and it's that way by design. He is the deceiver. THE deceiver. He has likely been the prince of deceit since before the Garden. How many centuries ago was that? Our minds can't even fathom how long he's been on this job. If we, as humans, can master something to the point of being titled an expert within a few years, how good is the enemy at deceiving us considering he's been doing it for thousands of years? A level of deceit my human mind can't quite understand. The tactics are subtle. It's the thought that lands on your mind of just "getting lunch" with that coworker after you've noticed how they look at you with lust in their eyes and a small part of you is intrigued by it. It's the little shoulder rub from the coworker when you're stressed out even though you know it's a step toward bad decisions. It's the tip toeing the line and flirting with boundaries when you know it could lead to infidelity. It's the doom scrolling on social media platforms to see profiles of people you find attractive knowing you already struggle with masturbation. It's going out for "one drink" knowing you have a habit of getting yourself in bad situations when you drink because you always go overboard. It's always seeking validation in private from men or women, knowing it will lead to bad decisions.

The enemy doesn't have to force us to do wrong. He simply tempts us. Furthermore, we all have to resist a common enemy, but we also have to resist our flesh. When we aren't sober we aren't vigilant. When we aren't vigilant we fall to the temptations that feed our fleshly desires. Once we've fallen, we know the feeling, we remember the rush, therefore we crave it even more than we did before we fell. It's a vicious cycle that will have you so dizzy you fail to see the only thing that will get you straightened out is seeking God to ask Him to set your path straight. This is why we see people stuck in destructive cycles for decades.

1 Peter 5: [8] Be sober-minded; be watchful. Your adversary the devil prowls around like a roaring lion, seeking someone to devour. [9] Resist him, firm in your faith, knowing that the same kinds of suffering are being experienced by your brotherhood throughout the world. [10] And after you have suffered a little while, the God of all grace, who has called you to his eternal glory in Christ, will himself restore, confirm, strengthen, and establish you.

Sober minded - Watchful - Resist him - Firm in faith - After you have suffered - God of all grace - Restore - Confirm - Strengthen - Establish.

I think being sober minded is about more than refraining from drunkenness or getting high on drugs. Think about the decisions you've made when you're lusting after someone, then think about the feeling you had after you got what you wanted from them and the rush went away. Did you regret it? Were you disappointed? Were you shameful? You felt that way after the fact because a mind set on lust is not a sober mind. Culture calls it "post nut clarity". In reality, it's sobriety. Think about the decisions you've made when you were angry, then think about how you felt after the rush went away and you had time to process the situation. Did you regret your decision? Were you embarrassed by how you acted? You felt that way because an angry mind is not a sober mind. One last example that we can all relate to; think about a time when you were upset and sad about something. What was that self talk like? Was it hyper pessimistic? Was it suicidal? Then think about how you felt when you were out of the slump and things were better for you. You probably looked back and asked yourself what got into you. Suicide over a situation that will come and pass? Coming into agreement with self hatred over something that will come and pass? It's because a depressed mind is not a sober mind. Anything that leads us to experience overwhelming emotions that result in beliefs contrary to what God says is nothing short of intoxication.

Desires of the eyes: It's never enough. As soon as you get what you wanted the feeling of satisfaction fades then you're on to the next thing that looks better to you. Nicer/more clothes, more Jewelry, more pretty women, more handsome men. This is like chasing the carrot. What we're looking for is illusive, it cannot be attained by ways of pursuit. The carrot will always be right out in front us.

Do you remember that time you went shopping for the perfect outfit to wear at the upcoming event? You bought it, put it on, took pictures, went out in it, posted pictures, soaked up the compliments, then forgot about that same exact outfit when the next outing came? That same outfit is probably in the back of your closet knowing good and well it will never be worn again. You remember that car you had to have? You got it, took pics of it, showed it off, drove it every chance you got, soaked up all the compliments but now that you've had it for a year and you see other people with it, you need the newest edition again?

Always having to purchase the "new". Always having to show off the material items you get before the people around you get them because you've made it part of your identity. These are things that mean nothing to the kingdom and clearly don't mean much to you considering your excitement for them dies just as fast as it came.

Matthew 6: 19 "Do not lay up for yourselves treasures on earth, where moth and rust destroy and where thieves break in and steal, 20 but lay up for yourselves treasures in heaven, where neither moth nor rust destroys and where thieves do not break in and steal. 21 For where your treasure is, there your heart will be also.

Matthew 6 is part of the Sermon on the Mount where Christ basically lays out ground rules for life, for those who want to be His follower. Before I was a believer I remember thinking God had all these rules and laws to keep us from enjoying life. Why can't I have premarital sex? What's wrong with focusing on getting rich all my life? Why can't I retaliate when someone does me wrong? Truth is, there is nothing God tells us TO DO or NOT TO DO to keep us from enjoying life, He gives us instruction to protect us and to lead us to a life that's truly worth living. It isn't enough to just not do the things He tells us not to do, we must live a consecrated life so that we may more clearly understand what He's calling us to do in this moment, this day and/or this season of life. If we spend our lives pursuing treasures of this earth we will spin our wheels until our dying days without ever experiencing fulfillment, love and confidence that we're truly fighting the good fight by His standard. How many times do we need to hear about a celebrity's self-destruction before we accept the sole pursuit of material items is a dead end? How many times do we need to hear the story about the man or woman who stood on the mountaintop of fame and worldly success then self-destructed in front of our faces before we accept that pursuit is a dead end? Do we really need to hear that story from another person to accept that God knows best and that we should surrender to His will for the life he gave us? When will we accept the real treasures of life are love, faith, Godly leadership, joy, peace, gentleness, kindness, goodness, self-control and most importantly, salvation? I'm not saying obtaining material items is a bad thing to desire. It isn't wrong to wear jewelry. It isn't wrong to upgrade cars. The fault comes when we make idols of material items and completely overlook the fact that those things mean little to nothing in the kingdom. These items surely should not be made part of our identity as God's creation. We have proof that material items aren't wrong to have throughout the Bible. Look how many faithful men of God were kings, leaders and had much influence within their communities. Focus on the things above. Your identity will be found in who you are in Christ, not material items.

Pride of life: The things we chase to prove ourselves we matter and that our lives are significant. Having to do something to try proving people wrong. To flaunt your material possessions to others in hopes you can convince them you're different or better. Flaunting success in your career, certain job titles, a partner that people find attractive, the size of your house, the make of your car etc. Pride is a disgusting sin. Pride will blind us from seeing the reality of our heart posture, leading to an inflated ego and a God complex. There are no good things that come from pride, unless a prideful soul repents and becomes a believer so that they may use their testimony to paint a picture of the destructive path pride leaves in an environment. Like the desires of the eyes, it's never enough. Pride is a bottomless pit that has to be fed at every possible opportunity. Every conversation has to be boosted by self-worship. Every relationship has to be boosted by frequent compliments, even if they're repetitive. Pride is the seed that every bad fruit bearing tree comes from. When people speak about generational curses they usually address things like addiction, sickness or poverty, but I believe the most common and overlooked "generational curse" is pride.

Pride looks like the "birthday queen" or "birthday king" that seems to think their birthday or birth week is a national holiday so they're repulsed by anyone who acts or thinks otherwise. Pride looks like the person that always has to let others know how "different" or "gifted" they are.

Pride looks like someone that can never see when they're in the wrong and since they can't see it, they can never admit it. Pride looks like someone reading this and thinking there is no pride within them.

A very sobering verse for those who understand the destruction pride has left or can leave in their life..

James 4:4 You adulterous people! Do you not know that friendship with the world is enmity with God? Therefore whoever wishes to be a friend of the world makes himself an enemy of God. 5 Or do you suppose it is to no purpose that the Scripture says, "He yearns jealously over the spirit that he has made to dwell in us"? 6 But he gives more grace. Therefore it says, "God opposes the proud but gives grace to the humble."

These three fleshly flaws keep us from living a consecrated life because they keep us focused on the world, they keep us focused on ourselves. One cannot serve two masters, so we have to seek intimacy with God daily in order to truly have intimacy with Him. There are three key things that come to mind when I think about consecration. From personal experience and biblical knowledge, I believe prayer, worship and fasting have been the most effective ways to consecrate. None of which are negotiable in my opinion. That said, there are seasons of life when you're more consistent with one than the others, so I don't think there is a perfect amount of time each day to dedicate time to each of these.

I'm not saying you can't have a relationship with Christ if you don't regularly pray, worship or fast, but I do believe your faith and desire to be obedient to Him will be minimal. Prayer, worship and fasting are mentioned all through the OT and NT. Christ addresses prayer and fasting in the Sermon on the Mount in a way that shows us there is no "if you want to pray" or "if you want to fast". This is what He says…

Matthew 7: [5] "And when you pray, you must not be like the hypocrites. For they love to stand and pray in the synagogues and at the street corners, that they may be seen by others. Truly, I say to you, they have received their reward. [6] But when you pray, go into your room and shut the door and pray to your Father who is in secret. And your Father who sees in secret will reward you.

Matthew 7: [16] "And when you fast, do not look gloomy like the hypocrites, for they disfigure their faces that their fasting may be seen by others. Truly, I say to you, they have received their reward. [17] But when you fast, anoint your head and wash your face, [18] that your fasting may not be seen by others but by your Father who is in secret. And your Father who sees in secret will reward you.

Christ says "WHEN" you pray and "WHEN" you fast, implying that to be a true follower of him these things are very highly recommended. Prayer will be discussed in another chapter, so I want to expand on biblical fasting a little. Christ gives instructions on how to carry ourselves when we fast, but we don't necessarily see instructions on what biblical fasting looks like, so we have to search the scriptures and do some research on how the Jews fasted during those times.

When we dig into the scriptures we see people like Moses, Elijah, Nehemiah, David, Daniel, Joel, Jesus, prophetess Anna and Paul were all intentional about fasting.

Moses - Exodus 34:28

Elijah - 1 kings 19:4-9

Nehemiah - Nehemiah 1:4

Daniel - Daniel 9:3

David - 2 Samuel 12:15-16

Joel - Joel 1:14-15 & Joel 2:12-17

Jesus - Matthew 4:1-3

Anna the prophetess - Luke 2:36-39

Paul - Acts 9:8-11

These fasts were for a multitude of reasons, but ultimately, the fasts were to receive instruction from God, receive mercy from God or done during a grieving period. There are also different types of jewish fasts, the most common are going without food and only drinking pure water or a dry fast, where no food or water was consumed. These are examples of biblical fasts. There is too much misunderstanding when it comes to fasting these days. Does God see you when you give up social media for a week? Yes, but that's not biblical fasting. Does God see you when you give up all meat except fish for a month? Yes, but that's not biblical fasting. The main point of fasting is to starve the flesh (some say crucify the flesh) so that the only strength and control you have during that period of time is given from God, which leads to the things mentioned above (Clarity for instruction, mercy and grieving). If you aren't uncomfortable physically while refraining from food or food and water, you won't truly see how intimacy with God through prayer, scripture reading, fellowship and worship will satisfy you. If you aren't experiencing that first hand, you're missing out on something miraculous God wants you to experience. Consecrate so you may come to an understanding of where God wants you to be in this moment or season he has given you. Consecrate so that your default is to consider the creator in all situations.

Romans 12 I appeal to you therefore, brothers, by the mercies of God, to present your bodies as a living sacrifice, holy and acceptable to God, which is your spiritual worship. [2] Do not be conformed to this world, but be transformed by the renewal of your mind, that by testing you may discern what is the will of God, what is good and acceptable and perfect.

The Old Testament points to Christ and reveals different parts of God's character that we need to know. Stop avoiding it.

CHAPTER 7

Personal Development and Self-Help

The personal development space has become more and more popular over the past decade which is both good and bad. We see this personal development doctrine everywhere on social media, podcasts and books. The perceived intention of the people who are prominent figures in the personal development space is to be a source of inspiration for those seeking to develop into a better version of themselves. Many people have followed these figures to get through weight loss journey's, build financial wealth, build businesses, get through breakups, divorces and many other life trials. Anyone who has been through a tough season of life understands the importance of being surrounded by people who care and will help lead through the chaos of life. Before I get into my beliefs on the personal development space, I have to make it clear that I'm not against positive influence at all. I find some of the personal development doctrine to be necessary for the betterment of society, especially men. Being that I worked in the fitness industry for 10 years, I was immersed in the personal development realm, as fitness is one of the key components of this new age personal development ideology. Most of my time in the industry was spent living by this ideology, but the Lord renewed my mind shortly after surrendering to Him.

From March of 2021 to February of 2026 I worked for a health and fitness company that had a backbone built on the personal development ideology I've mentioned. When I interviewed for the job it felt like a perfect fit for where my life was at the time. It was all about the betterment of myself so that I would be able to help others. I truly believe God put me in that environment to grow into a version of myself that would live sober long enough to eventually surrender my life to Him. When I started working for this company I was put in an entry level position where leadership had implemented a training system that had to be worked through before we were able to be promoted into higher level positions. There were 7 books throughout the different training tiers, all of which were focused on personal development and understanding human psychology as the primary way to persuade people to become loyal customers of your brand. I read each one of the books on the list and I felt like I was truly gaining wisdom that would lead me to achieve everything I ever wanted to achieve in life. The information felt ground breaking at the time, so I was thankful that the books were given to develop my work ethic, character and understanding of psychology.

Motivational speeches were another thing I was big on during that time. I spent a significant amount of time listening to different speakers around the world and taking notes from their speeches. With the combination of the personal development books and the motivational speeches, I was sure I was on the road to creating generational wealth and solving every problem I had in life.

Sometime in late 2022 I started to consider giving my life to Christ. I'm not exactly sure what led to this curiosity, but I do remember feeling like everything I believed about life was a lie, as I've always been what people would consider an intellect. It's as if the moment I started considering the creator on a daily basis, I transitioned from spending free time on personal development content to spending free time watching sermons on youtube. My curiosity turned into desire and excitement to hear pastors talk about the Bible. After I had spent months watching sermons, the free time I had eventually turned into daily scripture reading. The scripture reading turned into conversations and the conversations led to scripture studies and consistent deep dives into God's word. It didn't take long before I realized the Bible has many instructions that these personal development books have. The points weren't all exactly the same, but the "rules to live by" or "rules to success" were very similar to the biblical concepts I was reading about. Eventually, it became evident that these personal development books contain quotes that are either in line with scripture without giving God the glory or they're completely contrary to God's word. Many of them state Biblical principles with a worldly twist on them, which is really wild to me because these people are putting God's word in their books and making a profit off of them without ever acknowledging Him. Imagine living in a world that is so resistant to Christ that they intentionally rip Him off due to selfish ambition and continue living life acting as if they're the god everyone should follow.

Ecclesiastes 1:9 ESV
What has been is what will be,
and what has been done is what will be done,
and there is nothing new under the sun.

After coming to this realization, I couldn't help but see this everywhere within the personal development space. It's literally everywhere, in all the books, online courses and podcast episodes. Thankfully, I wasn't the only one to recognize it within my circle. There was an executive who worked for the company for close to 20 years, he was one of the most dedicated employees throughout the entire ecosystem. The type of guy that put all his value in what he could create out of his own strength by using what the world had to offer. This mindset led him to neglect close relatives and slowly chipped away at the relationship he had with his significant other. Around 2023 he was hit with a couple major life changes within a short period of time and eventually found the end of himself. During this time he came to a couple of our men's group Bible studies and opened up about where he was at mentally, which was a huge eye opener for those of us in the group. One of the things he mentioned that led him to opening the Bible on his own was going into a coworkers office one afternoon and seeing an open Bible sitting on the desk. He said he read a few verses and realized the personal development books he read in the past said very similar things, making this connection was one of the catalysts to the turning point in his life.

Once the realization was cemented, the Holy Spirit continued to sanctify him, it happened at such a rate he wasn't able to unsee what his eyes had been opened to within his life. After several months of contemplating, he ended up stepping down from his executive role then he eventually left the company. This man spent 60+ hours each week, for nearly 20 years, building a career he thought he would be proud of and quit after God opened his eyes. Getting to witness this season of his life play out from a distance is one of the most profound shifts I've ever witnessed. The" rara" personal development, nothing is ever good enough doctrine led to a dead end, but the good thing is, once God removes the scales and softens a heart he will allow us to keep the skills and lessons learned for the next season of life.

Romans 8:28 And we know that for those who love God all things work together for good, for those who are called according to his purpose.

I know there are influencers in the personal development space who lead with their faith in Jesus Christ, but I would say they're the minority. It seems most of the personal development space is full of influencers who resist God and choose to use his word and/or name for financial gain. There are some that will never mention God, you can listen to hours upon hours of their content and you'll never hear a genuine mention of God in any of it. I think some of the ones who claim to be believers but refuse to mention their faith in detail on their platforms are afraid of what people may think. They're afraid that if they incorporate faith in Christ it would deter people from watching, following and purchasing products or services so they stay far from it. They fear man more than they fear God. This is an example of idolatry. They idolize platforms, people, people pleasing, money and their idea of how their life is supposed to be. Not only is it idolatry, but their platforms are built on pride. These individuals operate in such a level of pride they think their way of life and what they consider "success" is more important than leading people to Christ, which is the ultimate success.

The crazy part about these types of influencers is, people will follow them as if they cracked some secret code. Due to the followers lack of knowledge they will follow the influencer as if they're the second coming of the messiah. It's no surprise though, considering this behavior was already prophesied.

2 Timothy 4:3 For the time is coming when people will not endure sound teaching, but having itching ears they will accumulate for themselves teachers to suit their own passions, 4 and will turn away from listening to the truth and wander off into myths.

Let me tell you something that could steer you in the right direction if you're in a season of looking for encouragement and inspiration. There is no better way to be encouraged than developing an intimate relationship with God and surrendering your life to Him. There is no better encouragement than asking God to let you see yourself for how He sees you instead of seeing yourself for how the world says you should see yourself. There is nothing more inspiring than reading about how God led men and their armies to victory, all by His strength even when they were the underdogs. There is nothing more inspiring than learning about how God used women to save and protect men time and time again throughout the scriptures. There is nothing that will lead you to success in this life like having a true, intimate, and personal relationship with Jesus Christ.

If you're seeking fulfillment, seek God. Do not fall into the trap of idolizing someone who spends their life resisting God. This type of individual will mislead you every time then produce content of how it's all your fault that you're falling short, as if they didn't convince you to buy all their courses on how to be "successful". They will lead you to hyper focus on the world instead of focusing on the things above. They will lead you to come into agreement with them and their philosophy instead of coming into agreement with the Kingdom of Heaven.

Matthew 23:25 "Woe to you, scribes and Pharisees, hypocrites! For you clean the outside of the cup and the plate, but inside they are full of greed and self-indulgence. 26 You blind Pharisee! First clean the inside of the cup and the plate, that the outside also may be clean.

If you're looking for personal development, the path is simple (not easy). Surrender your life to Jesus Christ because you cannot carry the burdens of life on your own and you definitely cannot fight the spiritual battles that have people bound to the ways of this world on your own.

Matthew 11:28-30 Come to me, all who labor and are heavy laden, and I will give you rest. 29 Take my yoke upon you, and learn from me, for I am gentle and lowly in heart, and you will find rest for your souls. 30 For my yoke is easy, and my burden is light."

Throughout the process of surrendering, study the scriptures deeply so that your mind may be renewed and set free from the world instead of being in agreement with the ways of the world.

John 8:31 So Jesus said to the Jews who had believed him, "If you abide in my word, you are truly my disciples, 32 and you will know the truth, and the truth will set you free."

This surrender and renewing of the mind will lead you to become a new version of yourself, a new creation. Becoming a new creation in Christ is more than just saying you believe in Jesus. A new creation sees the world differently, sees people differently,
has different preferences, has different desires, speaks different, thinks different and acts different.

2 Corinthians 5:17 Therefore, if anyone is in Christ, he is a new creation. The old has passed away; behold, the new has come.

I'm not saying earning more money or having financial goals is sinful. I'm not saying seeking personal development books and podcasts is a bad thing. I'm saying that we should be seeking understanding and relationship with God, our creator, to figure out what we're supposed to be doing with the life he's blessed us with. The personal development instruction is for micro doses of encouragement and critiquing work ethic, it's not supposed to be the laws to live by. Only the creator knows what the creation was made for. We should be seeking Him instead of idolizing popular influencers that are leading masses away from God in the name of personal development and success. How is someone who didn't create you and doesn't have a personal and public relationship with God going to convince you they know what you need to do to be successful in life? Success by who's standard? God is the one who decides whether we were successful in this life or not and we won't know for sure until it's all over.

I pray the men and women who have influence in the personal development space are able to see how their non biblical doctrine is deceptive to the people they're leading. I pray they're able to accept that they will be held accountable for how they led or misled God's people. I pray that the ones who have refused to surrender to Christ all these years make the decision to repent for deceiving God's children creating false idols out of selfish ambition. It went far beyond "help". It's a prime example of "blind leading the blind" and the enemy is masking it as "self help" because he knows if anyone tried to call out and correct the "self-help" industry they would be attacked and ridiculed for doing so. Wake up and peep the tactics.

For the ones who don't care at all, I pray God strips every material thing away from them that they consider to be good. I pray God exposes their deceitfulness and strips away every ounce of influence and every platform they've ever been placed on. I pray they find themselves laying naked on the ground, weeping, with not even a single blade of withered grass to hold onto to call theirs. I pray they grieve the loss of material items to the point that they're physically ill, day after day, until they reach a point of standing humbly before God with a repentant heart.

And I pray that one day God sees it fit to allow those repentant individuals to rebuild a platform that is built in His name so that they may use their testimony to lead people to Him. I pray those who experience this grief never forget the sovereignty of God. I pray that after they're built back up by the strength God gives them, they're able to forgive themselves for misleading God's people, as God forgives them at repentance. I pray they live the rest of life with a fear of God so great that they can't go a single day without seeking intimacy with Him. I pray they find joy in what came from the loss they experienced, understanding that it's better to have experienced it when they did, than to never have experienced it at all.

Christ and lucifer are not spiritual brothers. Scripture makes that very clear.

Chapter 8

Church Building Idolatry

(Webster Dictionary 1828) **CHURCH**, noun The collective body of Christians, or of those who profess to believe in Christ, and acknowledge him to be the Savior of mankind.

Church building idolatry looks like someone only praying, worshipping and serving if their church home leads them to do so. Church building idolatry looks like someone attending services and serving in the building but they never consider praying for a stranger in public or serving outside of the building. Church building idolatry looks like someone knowing God has put something on their heart to do for the kingdom but they ignore it because their church building doesn't approve.

Church building idolatry looks like someone serving the building at every chance they get with the assumption that it will earn them points in heaven.

Church building idolatry looks like someone being so hung up on their denominational doctrine that they can't associate and live life around people who attend different churches/claim different denominations.

Church building idolatry looks like someone proudly claiming their denomination instead of unapologetically claiming to be a follower of Christ.

Church building idolatry looks like someone allowing a new believer to stray from the Lord if the new believer doesn't

prefer their church, as if that ONE church building is the only option there is.
Church building idolatry looks like someone leading a non believer to think they can't be saved or learn about Christ if they don't attend a church.
Church building idolatry looks a lot like how THE church has been moving for as long as I can remember.

Yes, serving at the church you attend and being in fellowship with your "church family" is needed and appreciated, but it does not necessarily equate to salvation. I'm not anti church building. I believe finding a church home should be a priority for all believers, but that's not how someone's walk with Christ has to start. We've forgotten about The Great Commission, which is just as important today as it was on the day it was given.

Matthew 28:19

19 Go therefore and make disciples of all nations, baptizing them in the name of the Father and of the Son and of the Holy Spirit, 20 teaching them to observe all that I have commanded you. And behold, I am with you always, to the end of the age."

The verse says “Go therefore”, it doesn’t say “sit there and wait”. Go therefore and MAKE disciples. Some of us have been in the faith too long to be playing like a child in this walk. How does someone passively walk through the world seeing how bad it is then walk into a church building with their hands up on Sunday as if they’re really about that life? They’ve been calling themselves a follower of Christ for how many years? And their walk looks the exact same as it did on the day they surrendered? It’s because they think faith is about what they do when people are watching. It’s become a show to put on so they receive validation. The church building has been a place for people who live in fear to blend in instead of allowing it to develop them into a version of themselves that’s like a city on a hill that can’t be hidden.

We all (myself included) need to be praying that we do not fall into this trap of idolatry or idolatry of anything for that matter. We need to pray for steadfastness and boldness that can only be given by the Holy Spirit. We need to pray for the ability to see in others what the eyes cannot see so that we may be able to pray exactly what needs to be prayed over them. We need to pray that the boldness we’re given leads us to walk through this world as a light to others even after we make mistakes. We need to pray that the Lord allows us to see us how he sees us so that we may be confident of who we are IN CHRIST because if we don’t, the world will fill our minds with oppressive thoughts that lead to apathy and a life that lacks purpose. The battle continues after the Sunday service… and the majority, the most violent parts of the battle, are not inside of the church building.

I could see someone reading this and wondering what they can do to be more active for THE Church outside of the church building. My first piece of advice is to pray about it. Ask God to guide you in finding or creating ministry opportunities.

(Webster Dictionary 1828) **MIN'ISTRY**, noun Ecclesiastical function; agency or service of a minister of the gospel or clergyman in the modern church, or of priests, apostles and evangelists in the ancient.

We are blessed with many ways to minister the Gospel in most places. Ministry work stretches far beyond being a pastor or preacher. If you can give The Gospel, you can pray and you can love people, you have enough to reach the people God sent you here to reach. You may not be called to do it all on your own, so putting a team of people together who are on the same accord is necessary. That said, if you know you're supposed to do something for the Church on your own, do it. When trying to find ways to minister, consider things like food drives, worship and prayer events, adopt a family, neighborhood events, prayer walks, street evangelism, passing out bibles in public etc. The awesome thing about ministry is, God will allow us to use the skills we've developed in combination with the spiritual gifts he's given us to carry out certain ministries. Take your ideas to him. Ask for clarity, confirmation and instruction. We have to stop limiting God to a building a couple times a week. We aren't lacking in opportunities to spread the Gospel, to pray for people or to come together in worship with people from all different walks of life. The sick are out there and the sick still need a doctor.

“Everyone to whom much was given, of him much will be required..”

CHAPTER 9

Out of agreement. Into agreement.

If you were to start therapy the first few steps the therapist would walk you through is rapport, your reason for needing therapy and getting to know you by listening to you speak about life events. Their observation of how you explain things would allow them to gauge whether you've processed certain things or not. While they're listening they're looking for situations you were in that could lead to you having unpleasant beliefs about people, places, things or yourself. The most common verbiage we hear when it comes to these particular beliefs is "limiting beliefs". These are things we've come into agreement with that limit our mental capacity, skew our vision of life and skew the vision we have of ourselves. Not only do these limiting beliefs have an effect on how we see life, how we treat people, and how we allow people to treat us, but they also have an effect on our walk with Christ. We've all had experiences in life where we felt less than, if we dwelled on those thoughts too often we eventually came into agreement with a limiting belief. This process happens so subtly that many people end up living a majority of their lives in full agreement with the belief(s) without realizing it. These beliefs can be brought on by ourselves or it can be spiritually influenced (demonic oppression, influence or possession).

Examples of limiting beliefs are avoiding things you know you should do but you avoid them because you think you're bad at them. Things like public speaking, writing, tasks in the work place, relationships etc. Yes, it can be logical for you to be afraid of certain things, but the fear shouldn't cripple you from living the life you know God wants you to live (this can only be known through knowledge of scripture and intimacy with God).

Other, more serious limiting beliefs, would be things like believing no one loves you, your life will never get better, you don't deserve good things to happen to you or maybe you think people "like you" don't get to experience good things in life. These are all examples of limiting beliefs that were formed over time, through unpleasant experiences, negative self talk and/or spiritual oppression. My goal in this chapter is to open your mind to your limiting beliefs in hopes that you take them to God so he can renew your mind, which ultimately leads to freedom. What does it mean to come into agreement with something?

Luke 11:9-10 ESV

9 And I tell you, ask, and it will be given to you; seek, and you will find; knock, and it will be opened to you. 10 For everyone who asks receives, and the one who seeks finds, and to the one who knocks it will be opened.

These are the words of Christ as he was talking to his disciples. The key words in these verses are ask, seek and open. Living life with a biblical world view will allow us to see these verses for what they are, instructions from the Lord that will help us have intimacy with our heavenly father, leading to us being able to walk in the calling He has placed on our life. Contrarily, applying this concept to a secular world view can do the opposite. Hear me and think about how relatable this is to you when you look back on your life.

Ask: Most young minds aren't able to fully process life experiences and see them from different perspectives. We tend to focus so much on how we feel about things that we create a habit of seeing problems under a microscope instead of taking a step back to see more of what's really going on. When this happens we find ourselves looking for where we went wrong or trying to figure out what's wrong with us. This is a process that happens within the depths of our mind, never really getting outside for our loved ones to help us process our thoughts. So, you're ASKING yourself what's "wrong" with YOU and once you can think of something that makes sense, you stick with it.

Seek: Once you think you've identified what your problems are, you subconsciously look for things to validate the belief. You unintentionally SEEK reasons to be right because it's the only thing that makes sense within your framework. We love to seek a sense of understanding even if what we're telling ourselves isn't true understanding. We will be content with believing a lie as long as it validates the thoughts hidden deep in our mind.

Open: When we've found ways to justify sticking to the belief, we've officially come into agreement with the limiting beliefs. Our minds are CLOSED to the possibility that we may be wrong, which ultimately OPENS us up to more self criticism because it's more validation for the limiting beliefs. This is why someone who is in a depressive state unloads an overwhelming amount of problems on the person they're venting with. The root of the depression started with a single thought, then it all spiraled downhill from there, limiting belief stacking on top of limiting belief and feeding the other limiting beliefs. In my experience, it's rare that someone venting to me is struggling with one single belief that has them living in fear, it's always a chain of pessimism.

We're always coming into agreement with something whether it's intentional or unintentional. I'm gonna give you an experience I had growing up that led to the limiting belief or the "agreement " I've lived with for over a decade. This experience led to beliefs that limited my capacity to see life how God wants me to see it and to see myself how God wants me to see myself. I've been through seasons of therapy two different times in my life, so I want to make it clear that I'm not against therapy. I actually believe everyone should prioritize therapy at some point. Not just any therapy though, I believe we should find a therapist we connect with, and we should go in person because that is how one would benefit most if they're truly seeking knowledge on how to heal. That said, this particular situation is something the Holy Spirit revealed to me after I prayed and asked for understanding of what limiting beliefs I have about myself that keep me from walking in the calling He has placed on my life.

See, therapy isn't the only way to find out what's going on within. God created us and He created every person that we've encountered in this life, He created every bit of nature we see, plus the stars, the sun, the moon, and so on. Why would we ever think that we can't go to Him to get answers on what we need to know about ourselves? Before I get into this life experience, I need to preface it; scripture tells us to not be conformed to the ways of the world, but to be transformed by the renewing of our minds… I think most people would mention things like alcoholism, drug addiction, premarital sex and/or a life of crime if they were to be asked to give examples of what it means to be "conformed to the ways of the world". Yes, those are ways that we can be conformed to the ways of the world, but there are so many other ways that we, as believers, and followers of Jesus Christ, have been conformed to the world. Simply thinking we have to go to a therapist to find out what's going on inside of us is a prime example of our mind being conformed to the ways of the world. Why are we only searching for what the world has to offer when it comes to healing? Really think about that. The world has made us believe we can only seek what's within it instead of going to the God that created the world and every living thing in it. For the sake of being able to walk in the calling God has placed on your life, I encourage you, please come out of agreement with that belief right now. He has more to offer and it's literally out of this world.

As I mentioned before, I was raised by my grandparents until I was 13. They lived a very simple life here in the Midwest. To them life was mostly about working and spending time with family. They didn't seem to be focused on anything more than that, which is perfectly fine if that's all you ever wanted, but as a young boy I wanted to have fun. I wanted to enjoy life as a normal kid. My first aspiration in life was to be an athlete.

Growing up, I wanted to play basketball more than anything. We had a goal and a concrete slab in front of our trailer where I spent a lot of time shooting around before I even knew anything about the sport. I remember the high school would have camps during a few weekends throughout the summer, so I would go anytime I got the chance. Those camps were probably the first thing I ever thoroughly enjoyed as a child. I always gave my full effort and I was always locked in so I could learn something new. The problem was, my grandparents didn't care about my aspirations. To them, me going to one of those camps was just a weekend of fun that I would get to have every once in a while, they didn't realize how much I really wanted to play and they didn't find it necessary to spend money on things like skills training, basketball shoes or anything else that comes with raising a young athlete. Their perspective on life was to make good grades in school then get a job after you graduated, they weren't the type of people to dream of anything more in life. My sports career as a young athlete started when I got into the eighth grade. After my aunt and uncle took me in they did everything they could to push me into new hobbies so I could enjoy life and have more fulfillment as a teenager. My 8th grade year was the first season I played a sport for the school district. I was actually a standout player and known in the district for being a solid defensive player. Because of my new found athletic career and acceleration in basketball, I started gaining popularity in school. Man, I went from being angry and depressed to living life on a high. This was the first time I was ever known for something good amongst my peers. Prior to this all I was ever known for was fighting and making bad grades. My life experience had significantly changed just by becoming an athlete and pouring time and energy into something productive. It's amazing what sports can do for a young person, especially when mentors are around them, pouring into them and speaking life into them. For the adults reading this, please never overlook the power of your words and the intentional time you give to a young person, it can save their life.

My claim to fame as a young athlete only lasted through eighth grade. I grew faster than everyone so I was always one of the taller kids on the team, which is why I played 4 and 5. When I moved up into high school I was no longer a big, so my positions transitioned from a 4 and 5 to playing at 2 and 3. Man, this was an unexpected change for me. Not only was I an underclassman, but I was also put into a new position on the court and I was not prepared.

As I mentioned before, this is also about the time that I was getting into frequent partying. The time I should've been putting into skills training, nutrition, and more intentional strength training that was catered to being a hooper, I spent trying to fit in by taking part in extracurricular activities that had nothing to do with basketball. The lack of buy-in on my part led to me being trash in the sport my freshman and sophomore year. I sat the bench every game and only went in during a blowout game. All of this led to a lot of negative self talk and took a toll on my confidence as a young man. I'm sure many of you experienced something like this throughout your years in school. You tried a sport, you played it for a few years, but you were never truly good at it. Not only was I a young man that wasn't good at something he set out to do, I was also the only athlete in the school district that was black, so I caught a lot of slack for not fitting the stereotype of being good at basketball.

Right before the first tournament of my junior season I tore my ACL and meniscus while at practice. This was pretty devastating because I just became an upperclassman and had actually put in more time than ever skills training and working out. I went through all the rehabilitation to get my physical performance back. Once I was back to that 90% point I was in the gym training again. Eventually, I got to a point where I was better than ever, not so much physically, but with the aspects of the sport all around. I was a better shooter, had better IQ, I dealt with pressure better, and I was better at handling the ball up and down the court.

Going into my senior season I expected to get a lot more playing time. Practices were going well for me at first. I was performing well, and my teammates recognized it very early on, but it seemed like my coaches didn't care. When we scrimmaged I performed well on the court, but I was still sitting the bench quite a bit, which did not sit well with me considering all the work I put in to rehabilitate and improve my performance. On top of my frustration for sitting the bench during practice, I had a bad attitude and was being pulled between becoming the life of the party and being a student that focused on the important things. One evening after sitting the bench at practice I went to the locker room, grabbed my jersey and set it on the coaches desk. I was done. How dare my Coach not acknowledge the work I put in during the off-season. My pride couldn't handle it so I quit and decided to dedicate my time to the party life.

To you, as a reader, this may not seem like anything significant whatsoever, and to be honest I really didn't think it was either. When I used to think back on it, it just seemed like the common teenager struggle. It didn't seem like anything that would really have much of an effect on me in my adulthood. But God proved me wrong.

About a year ago, I started really looking into **deliverance ministry**. I kept hearing the same phrase over and over "come into agreement" or "come out of agreement", so I started looking into what it is to come into or out of agreement with something. Someone recommended me to take certain things I was struggling with to God, so I started to say things in prayer like "Holy Spirit, if there is anything in my life that I have come into agreement with, whether intentionally or unintentionally, please reveal it to me and lead me to do what I need so that I can come out of agreement with it". Once I started praying like that, there were so many things that would come to mind, all of which the Lord has helped me walk-through so that I can fully process and lay it at his feet. The basketball one has taken some time though. With this particular process, I was hit with dreams three nights in a row. All three dreams were me playing basketball and playing like absolute trash. After the third night of having a basketball dream I sat up out of bed and asked the Holy Spirit why I kept having these dreams. At that point in time I hadn't played in several months, so it didn't make sense for me to consistently have basketball specific dreams.

One morning I was on a prayer walk and the Holy Spirit revealed to me that I needed to process the beliefs that were formed throughout that period of my life. The beliefs that were directly correlated to basketball season. This is ultimately what led me to see that the years of scrutiny and struggle I dealt with during that time stuck with me into adulthood. The limiting beliefs kept me from being confident with anything I did in front of groups of people. They kept me from being confident at picking up new things like writing and speaking. They kept me from truly having fun playing games or sports because I was afraid to suck at something again, so I would end up being over competitive.

This probably isn't something I ever would've mentioned to my therapist when it came to taking the steps to heal because, like I mentioned before, I didn't think it held much significance. That's why we must take our grievances and our past struggles to God. It doesn't matter how many degrees and accolades a psychologist has, their knowledge is far inferior to His knowledge. Is it possible that I could still live an obedient life and walk in the calling the Lord has placed on my life? Maybe. That said, God is good and because He is good He has good reasons for the things he does.

He clearly wanted me to address that period of my life head on so that He can help me deal with it properly. The burden that is lifted off of us when we go to Him for healing is something words can't quite describe.

Furthermore, the importance of asking the Lord to remove burdens so that we may be able to continue walking in obedience also cannot be described, you just have to experience it to see.

Ask Him to

1. Reveal what you need to know. Reveal what you haven't been seeing.
2. Lead you through a process to come out of agreement with the lies and come into agreement with what He says about you.

Romans 12:1-2 ESV

12 I appeal to you therefore, brothers, by the mercies of God, to present your bodies as a living sacrifice, holy and acceptable to God, which is your spiritual worship. 2 Do not be conformed to this world, but be transformed by the renewal of your mind, that by testing you may discern what is the will of God, what is good and acceptable and perfect.

Romans 8:1-11 ESV

8 There is therefore now no condemnation for those who are in Christ Jesus. 2 For the law of the Spirit of life has set you free in Christ Jesus from the law of sin and death. 3 For God has done what the law, weakened by the flesh, could not do. By sending his own Son in the likeness of sinful flesh and for sin, he condemned sin in the flesh, 4 in order that the righteous requirement of the law might be fulfilled in us, who walk not according to the flesh but according to the Spirit. 5 For those who live according to the flesh set their minds on the things of the flesh, but those who live according to the Spirit set their minds on the things of the Spirit. 6 For to set the mind on

the flesh is death, but to set the mind on the Spirit is life and peace. 7
For the mind that is set on the flesh is hostile to God, for it does not
submit to God's law; indeed, it cannot. 8 Those who are in the flesh
cannot please God. 9 You, however, are not in the flesh but in the
Spirit, if in fact the Spirit of God dwells in you. Anyone who does not
have the Spirit of Christ does not belong to him. 10 But if Christ is in
you, although the body is dead because of sin, the Spirit is life
because of righteousness. 11 If the Spirit of him who raised Jesus
from the dead dwells in you, he who raised Christ Jesus from the
dead will also give life to your mortal bodies through his Spirit who
dwells in you.

Every thought is not yours. Every financial come up is not from God. Every hardship is not of the enemy.

CHAPTER 10

Thoughts on prayer

Prayer is powerful. I think we can all agree, the believers and the non-believers, which is a weird statement to make, but I think it's true. Humans have an innate understanding of the need for prayer. Anytime we intentionally go to the Lord with questions, grievances, praise, or anything else we have hope that He hears us. I want to take a deeper dive into a few different things along the lines of prayer that the Lord has revealed to me throughout my walk.

What is prayer?

(Webster Dictionary 1828) **PRA'YER**, noun In worship, a solemn address to the Supreme Being, consisting of adoration, or an expression of our sense of God's glorious perfections, confession of our sins, supplication for mercy and forgiveness, intercession for blessings on others, and thanksgiving, or an expression of gratitude to God for his mercies and benefits. A prayer however may consist of a single petition, and it may be extemporaneous, written or printed.

Many times, especially early in our walk, we go only to God to ask him for things. We treat Him as if he's a genie which ultimately reveals our heart posture, and our lack of understanding of who the God of the Bible is. If you go through your walk with the mindset of only seeking response from God when you need something you are missing out on a lifetime of sanctification, fulfillment and whatever else He planned for you before He made you in your mothers womb. I believe there are many reasons why faith in the United States looks so different from faith in the east, and one of those reasons is a weak prayer life. If we don't study God's word we aren't aware of all the things He has done for people, to people and through people since the beginning of time. Both the Old Testament and the New Testament reveal the different characteristics of God in a way that lead us to see there isn't anything he cannot do. Coming to somewhat of an understanding of the sovereignty, power, omnipresence, love and faithfulness of God is crucial to having a consistent and genuine prayer life. I say "somewhat" because I don't believe it's possible for us to fully grasp the depth of God, but if we can study, if we can be in fellowship and hear testimonies enough, we can get to a point of understanding that will have a tremendous impact on our life.

Outside of daily scripture reading and Bible studies, googling things like "names given to God in scripture" helped me get more of an understanding of God's character. With a quick search you can find many names for God along with the meanings of those names, which is where the breakthrough happened for me. Here are a few names you'll see..

Yahweh - I AM (Exodus 3:14. "Yahweh" is Hebrew for "I AM" signifying ultimate self sufficiency)

Immanuel - God is with Us (Name given in Isaiah 7:14. Hebrew for "God with us")

El Roi - God who sees me (Genesis 16:13. El Roi is Hebrew for "the God who sees")

Jehovah Jireh - God our provider (Genesis 22:14. "Jireh" is Hebrew for "will provide")

Jehovah Rapha - Lord the healer (Exodus 15:26. "Rapha" is Hebrew for "to heal")

Jehovah Nissi - The Lord my banner (Exodus 17:15. "Nissi" is Hebrew for "my banner")

Jehovah Shalom - The Lord is peace (Judges 6:24. "Shalom" is Hebrew for "peace")

Jehovah Raah - The Lord is my shepherd (Psalm 23. "Raah" is Hebrew for "shepherd")

Alpha & Omega - The beginning and end of all things (Revelation 1:8, 21:6 & 22:13)

God of Abraham, Isaac & Jacob (Exodus 3:15)

Christ

Spotless lamb/ Lamb without blemish - (1 Peter 1:19)

King of kings, Lord of lords - (Revelation 19:16)

The way, the truth, the life (John 14:6)

Oftentimes I start my prayers with addressing God by these names. Doing this helps me recall all the amazing things he has done. Whether I'm in a season of struggle, a season of victory or a season of uncertainty, saying these things reminds me that he can do all things. Hallelujah. Him and Him only.

It's become evident that prayer is a common struggle point amongst believers, not just new believers, but believers in all different areas of their walk with Christ. I've noticed many people are nervous to pray in small groups, so they attend the group for months on end, never praying over their community. This may be an example of a limiting belief. If someone doesn't believe they also have the freedom to go to God in prayer, they won't and they'll be afraid to open up about the fact that they don't know what to say when they pray. This mindset is what allows for a weak prayer life. I've seen people get so nervous that all they can say is "dear God… I don't know what to say". I've witnessed this so many times while being in fellowship and it grieves me every time because people are being crippled by fear and lack of understanding, which can hinder them from breaking strongholds, receiving revelation, interceding for others, developing intimacy with God and receiving instruction. Identifying this issue led me to create a framework to help people be more intentional about developing their prayer life. This exact framework or structure is not law, so you won't find it in scripture but it is useful for helping someone become more comfortable with prayer, not only in their private time, but in small groups as well. For the new believer or cultural christian that's not in the word, understand that the most important instruction for prayer is the Lord's Prayer given by Christ himself, so I'll lay that out then get into the framework that has helped my prayer life.

If you break this prayer down you'll see there is intentionality for how the prayer is said. Addressing God for who He is, praising His name, acceptance of His will above all, acknowledgement of His sovereignty in heaven and on earth, acceptance of our dependency on Him to provide for us, seeking repentance, and asking for His divine protection.

Matthew 6:9 Pray then like this: "Our Father in heaven,
hallowed be your name.
10 Your kingdom come,
your will be done,
on earth as it is in heaven.
11 Give us this day our daily bread,
12 and forgive us our debts,
as we also have forgiven our debtors.
13 And lead us not into temptation,
but deliver us from evil.

For your more personal and detailed prayers when it comes to what you experience throughout your day to day, here is a structure that will help.

Recall who He is and what He has done

As I mentioned before, this is a great way to start your prayers because it reminds you of all the things He has done. You may not know a bunch of different scriptures off the top of your head where He did miraculous and unfathomable things, but you at least know a couple, you definitely know the things he has done in your life. What you recall doesn't have to be anything extreme either, it could simply be something like someone giving you a free Bible at a peculiar time in life, protecting you from troubles you could have been part of but He redirected you, or how he laid the foundation of the Earth in such a beautiful way. Don't rush this part of the prayer. You can sit in silence as long as you need. As you sit in silence things will come to mind that you can give him praise for which will lead to feeling strengthened and hopeful by considering his grace, sovereignty and unfailing plan for creation. There is no set time I recommend for this, just do what feels right in the moment. One day you might only spend 20 seconds in this portion, the next day you may spend 20 minutes in this portion, I think it depends on the season of life you're in or how your day is going.

Sit in silence and wait for the instruction

This period of silence is not set to a specific amount of time. It may take five seconds for you to receive something or five minutes, I believe this is a necessary discipline for strengthening your prayer life. The point is to pray for whoever and whatever comes to mind that does not pertain to you. For example, maybe after sitting in silence for a few seconds, you think about the cashier you had a brief conversation with at the grocery store that day. Lift them up in prayer and pray for whatever comes to mind in that moment, think about the human experience, think about how you felt when you looked that person in the eye, think about their delivery when they spoke to you. Reflecting on all those things will help you see potential areas of their life that you could pray for. Continue to sit in silence and allow the Holy Spirit to download things on your mind so that you may pray for whoever comes up. This is usually the longest portion of my prayer. Don't overlook the power of intercession. Do not rush this process, and when the spirit puts someone on your mind, be sure you don't disregard, pray for them even if it doesn't make sense. Maybe you haven't spoken to them in years, pray for them anyway. Maybe you're mad at them or you're harboring resentment in your heart toward them, pray for them anyway, then pray for your own heart. Maybe they told you everything is going well in their life, pray for them anyway. Maybe someone pops up in your mind that you never met, pray for them anyway.

Now talk to Him about YOU

Take your request to him. Take your grievances to him. Take your questions to him. Ask him to reveal the secrets of heaven to you so that you may understand him and the calling He has placed on your life more. Ask the Holy Spirit to probe your life and reveal the things you need to address. Ask him how to handle what he reveals to you. Ask him to show you how to handle things like relationships, finances, gifts, and time. Ask Him for forgiveness and ask Him to lead you through repentance.

(Webster Dictionary 1828 - **Repentance** - sorrow or deep contrition for sin, as an offense and dishonor to God, a violation of his holy law, and the basest ingratitude towards a Being of infinite benevolence. This is called evangelical *repentance* and is accompanied and followed by amendment of life.)

Some circumstances won't allow you to go this in depth during prayer time, but when you have as much time as you need this framework will help strengthen your prayer life significantly.

Group prayers are my favorite. Brothers and sisters in Christ coming together on the same accord is a very powerful thing. We get glimpses of this in Genesis and throughout the book of acts. The Book of Acts shows us how instructions from God are made clear, danger is avoided and buildings can literally shake when believers come together on the same accord.

The tower of Babel is also a great example of what can happen when people come together on the same accord.

Genesis 11:4-8

4 Then they said, "Come, let us build ourselves a city and a tower with its top in the heavens, and let us make a name for ourselves, lest we be dispersed over the face of the whole earth." 5 And the Lord came down to see the city and the tower, which the children of man had built. 6 And the Lord said, "Behold, they are one people, and they have all one language, and this is only the beginning of what they will do. And nothing that they propose to do will now be impossible for them. 7 Come, let us go down and there confuse their language, so that they may not understand one another's speech." 8 So the Lord dispersed them from there over the face of all the earth, and they left off building the city.

We, human beings, set out to build a tower from the ground all the way up to the heavens. God, the creator of all, had to put a stop to it because human beings came together on the same accord and were so effective when they set out to do something. The issue likely was, the further building of the tower would've led to many casualties because it was dangerous and it was outside of God's will. If they were that effective at carrying out plans by their own strength, what happens when God calls a group of people together to put them on an assignment? What happens when the entire group is on the same accord in prayer and supplication? The task at hand will be completed no matter how far out of reach it seems. God isn't the one lacking power or a plan, the Church has to surrender and move according to His will.

We have to seek Him, and accept that faith, community and endurance are needed to fulfill what He has created us and sent us here for.

Acts 4:31 And when they had prayed, the place in which they were gathered together was shaken, and they were all filled with the Holy Spirit and continued to speak the word of God with boldness.

A group of believers all together, on the same accord, during a time of extreme persecution, had so much faith and such a desire to further the Gospel that the physical building shook. They continued to gather together and spread the gospel, making converts in their communities and creating disciples across the nations, despite the fact that believers were being martyred right in those very communities. God will guide, God will provide. God will protect. God will see to it that we complete what he ordained us to do no matter what the current atmosphere is.

Church services matter, worship events matter, prayer events matter. Whether the services and events are only a few people, a few hundred people or a few thousand people, everyone being on the same accord is extremely important. Yes, God hears the prayers of one person and will answer them, but there's something extraordinary about ordinary people coming together in supplication. When someone is praying over you, don't just listen, be intentional about being in agreement with their prayer. When you're sitting in a service or event and someone is praying, don't just listen, be intentional about being in agreement with their prayer. Let's not fall into the cycle of checking boxes and passively speaking to the creator or all things. Pray like you're talking and listening to God.

If the religion was built on a false prophet the entire religion is false.

Outro

Thank you for making it this far in my book. I hope you were able to get something from these life experiences, scriptures and pieces of my mind. I truly believe each and every one of us could impact lives in the most positive way if we would just be vulnerable and share what we got from our experiences. God gives us a story and sharing that story matters. You may feel like it's boring or maybe you feel like you're not important enough to share a testimony and change someone's life, but your story is capable of doing that. All of us, and I mean all of us, have been through trials or are currently experiencing blessings we've prayed for. The power is in testifying how God delivered you from the things that manifested in your life after those experiences. The power is in sharing your testimony and explaining to people how God delivered you from addiction, depression, alcoholism, witchcraft, idolatry, false religion, prostitution, a life of crime, etc. He may not communicate with you the same way he does with me, but he is trying to communicate with you. You may not have been through the exact same experiences but hopefully you can apply my take-aways, along the scriptures provided, to your circumstances in order to see Him in the midst of all of it.

Maybe you're still living in these things. I'm here to tell you, if you really want change and you're willing to surrender, God will hear you when you call. He will reveal himself to you if you ask Him, I've heard countless testimonies where he did exactly that for those who asked him. Since you're in the slump right now, I'm not gonna sugarcoat it, it sucks. I'm sure you have days when you've woken up and you didn't want to be here and maybe you even have nights when you lay down in bed and you hope you don't wake up. I've been there and millions of other people out there have been there as well. You don't want to die, you just don't want to live life feeling how you feel right now. There are better days ahead. The best nugget of information I can give you is this; if only I had known all the trials I was going through would eventually give me a perspective on life that allows me to help people reconsider their purpose, the grief in the moment would've been so much easier to handle. There comes a time when you look back and it all makes sense, even if it still hurts a little. Everything will be alright, things are just a little uncomfortable right now.

If you're reading this in a season of thriving, be sure to thank God everyday. Never go back to the old you, but at the same time, never forget it. When you meet someone who is going through what you've been through, take the time to sit with them as a human being to hear them out and encourage them. Sometimes a listening ear without a verbal response is all someone needs to know their existence matters. Never forget that.

I encourage you to steward what you've been given and prepare yourself to steward what you know God is planning to give you. Steward your health. Steward your relationships. Steward your finances. Steward the skills you've been blessed enough to develop. Steward the gifts He's given you. Steward your time.

Acknowledgments

I have to give credit to so many people for being part of and caring about my life. First and foremost, I thank my mother for going against the grain of what the people closest to her wanted, for deciding not to get an abortion. Not only that, but she went through a life of trials I couldn't imagine going through and still had the heart to give birth to my sister, Samantha, four years before I was born. From the bottom of my heart, thank you.

Now for my sister, Samantha… Thank you for always being there to defend me, thank you for always being there to lead me, thank you for always being there to feed me, thank you for always being there to comfort me, thank you for making me a priority in your life even when I didn't appreciate it and thank you for giving me a niece and nephew. Even up until this point in my life there is no one closer to my heart than you. I'm beyond grateful for your existence.

For the grandparents who raised me, Samantha and Ginny, thank you for welcoming us with open arms. Thank you for taking on responsibilities you never asked for. Thank you for enduring those tough days of working your job, trying to take care of a family and trying to take care of yourself. For my grandma Chris, thank you for doing what you could to continue taking care of us kids even after your husband passed. To say I'm grateful for you parenting me the first

13 years of my life would be an understatement. Thank you.

There are so many other people I owe more than thanks to but I'll start with this. To my dear aunt and uncle that took Samantha and I in when I was 13, thank you. Both of you have since left to be with the Lord, but it didn't feel right to do this outro without mentioning both of you.

To all my other aunts and uncles that played a role in my upbringing, whether it was babysitting for a couple hours, taking me hunting and fishing, cooking meals for me or just visiting and spending time with the family, thank you. To my grandma Theresa and my grandpa Gary, I could write an entire book trying to describe my appreciation, but I'll keep it short and hope that you hear my heart when reading this, thank you for always being there and caring about Samantha and I. Thank you for all the long drives from Texas to Missouri just to spend time with the family. Thank you for always telling the truth no matter how uncomfortable it was. Thank you for being open to having conversations with me in order to mend our relationship. From the bottom of my heart, thank you so much.

To all the teachers I had who tolerated my bad attitude and continued to give me grace, thank you so much. I still remember many of you from elementary, middle and high school. The roles you played, not only in my life, but in the lives of hundreds of students who sit in your classrooms matters so much more than you could ever imagine.

To family friends and extended family like Chris and Kiley Rigdon, Kenny and Shelly Buxton, Shorty and Summer, grandma Jimmy and grandpa Rick, Vernon and Angie Boen, Shelly Bryant, Stacy McLain, Lonnie Eaton, Ken and Deanna Gidden, Jim and Linda Sitez, the Hammer's family, and everyone else that was ever there to show me love in anyway, thank you so much.

Thank you to my brothers and sisters in Christ. The Lord has put so many of you in my life. Jarrett and Becky Bond, Evan and Jordan Johnson, Nolan and Jan Manning, Kado, Tom Carter, Terik, Damion, Jaime, James Futrell, Lex Burton, Arionna Butler, Cynthia Okoulatsongo, Madison Simmons, Leslie Taylor, Chaz and Maddy Mcdonald, Jaredd Williams, Kate Brennan, Kait Soihl, Alex Meadows, Isaiah Goesman.

For anyone I've forgotten, please forgive me, the Lord has been good to me for as long as I can remember so it's hard to name everyone at the moment.

I pray for protection and a life worthy of inheriting the Kingdom of Heaven for each and every one of you.

- Micah

Psalm 23

The LORD is my shepherd; I shall not want. 2 He
makes me lie down in green pastures.
He leads me beside still waters. 3 He restores my
soul.
He leads me in paths of righteousness
for his name's sake. 4 Even though I walk
through the valley of the shadow of death, I will
fear no evil,
for you are with me; your rod and your staff,
they comfort me. 5 You prepare a table before
me in the presence of my enemies; you anoint
my head with oil;
my cup overflows. 6 Surely goodness and mercy
shall follow me all the days of my life, and I shall
dwell in the house of the LORD forever.

Made in the USA
Coppell, TX
14 June 2026

81584574R00080